Crochet Amigurumi Baby Animals

Patterns to Create Adorable Critters Animal Friends

COMPLETE GUIDE TO CROCHET TOYS TECHNIQUES MADE EASY

Volume 3
Patterns by Kristi Tullus

Edit by

Publish by

ISBN: 9781802210057

Content

Deer ... page 3
Reindeer ... page 16
Raccoon ... page 30
Small Donkey ... page 42
Christmas Teddy ... Bear 52
Long-Legged Bunny ... page 64

essential stitches tips
Crochet Stitches ... page 71
Amigurumi Essentials ... page 72

Crochet pattern by Kristi Tullus

Size

27 cm (10 2/3") from head to toe, with DK weight alpaca wool and a 2,50 mm hook.

Skills required

Crocheting in spiral, slip stitch, single crochet stitch, increasing and decreasing.

Difficulty

3. Intermediate – includes some less common crochet techniques and color changes.

Contact Info

Pattern includes unlimited support from me over email or Skype. Crochet photo and video tutorials and helpful tips are available on my website.

 kristi@spire.ee    http://sidrun.spire.ee    a0kristi

Copyright © 2016 TÜ Spire. Contents of this document MAY NOT be copied, reproduced, altered, published or distributed in any way. You MAY sell finished products made with this pattern, provided you credit me as the designer (KristiTullus, http://spire.ee/).

Tip! You can use the same pattern to make larger or smaller toys by using finer or bulkier yarn. Make sure to pick a crochet hook at least a size smaller than suggested on the yarn label and crochet tightly enough to achieve a tight gauge that will not allow the stuffing to show through the fabric. You may also need to adjust the size of the safety eyes, nose and joints.

Materials & Tools

- Yarn. I used DK weight alpaca yarn, 100 m = 50 g (109 yd = 50 g) / 8 ply / 11 wpi / 3: light. You will need about 95 g of beige, 15 g of brown and 10 g of white yarn.
- 2,50 - 3,50 mm crochet hook (US size 2/C - 4/E) or according to the yarn.
- Polyester fiberfill, wool, wadding for stuffing.
- 12 mm (1/2") safety eyes or buttons, beads, felt etc.
- Two 20 mm (3/4") and two 15 mm (3/5") doll joints or safety eyes or buttons and thread.
- Embroidery floss.
- Yarn needle, scissors, stitch marker.

Choosing joints

Tip! You can use plastic doll joints, cotter pin joints, buttons and thread or even just thread to attach the arms and legs. My favorite are plastic doll joints - they are easy to install, durable and washable. Buttons and thread will work great as well, if you can't get your hands on any joints.

Plastic doll joints

1. Plastic doll joints come in three pieces - disk with a stem, washer and a fastener.

2. Disk with a stem is placed inside the limbs, pushing the stem through the fabric.

3. And then locked to place inside the body.

Button and thread joints

Tip! Make sure you use a very strong thread to attach the limbs – it will have to endure quite a bit of tension and can be a bit difficult to mend, should it break. I have found cotton embroidery floss, nylon sewing thread (doubled or tripled) or fishing line work really well.

1. Cut a length of yarn and draw it through the holes in the button.

2. Place the button inside a limb, drawing the yarn tails through the fabric.

3. Place the other button inside the body, draw the yarn tails through the holes and knot them together.

Abbreviations

- st(s) = stitch(es).
- mr, sc *n* = crochet *n* (number) single crochet stitches in to the adjustable loop (see page 14).
- ch = chain stitch.
- sl st = slip stitch (single crochet stitch in UK and Australia).
- sc = single crochet stitch (double crochet stitch in UK and Australia).
- sc (or sl st, ch, hdc etc.) *n* = make *n* single crochet stitches (or sl st, ch, hdc etc.), one in each stitch.
- inc = increase – crochet two single crochet stitches in the same stitch.
- dec = decrease – crochet two stitches together using the invisible decrease method (see page 15).
- (sc 4, inc) x *n* = repeat the pattern between parentheses *n* times.
- (36) = number of stitches in a round after finishing round.

Notes

- Work in a continuous spiral, do not join rounds or turn your work, unless instructed otherwise in the pattern.
- Work all stitches in both loops, unless instructed otherwise in the pattern.
- Make sure to crochet tightly enough to achieve a tight gauge that will not allow the stuffing to show through the fabric.
- Use a stitch marker or a piece of yarn to mark the end or the beginning of a round. Move the marker up after completing each round.

Head

With beige yarn:

1: mr, sc 6	(6)
2: inc x 6	(12)
3: (sc, inc) x 6	(18)
4: (inc, sc 2) x 6	(24)
5: (sc 7, inc) x 3	(27)
6: sc in each st	(27)
7: sc 3, inc, (sc 8, inc) x 2, sc 5	(30)
8: sc in each st	(30)
9: (sc 9, inc) x 3	(33)
10: sc in each st	(33)
11: sc 4, inc, (sc 10, inc) x 2, sc 6	(36)

On round 12 place a stitch marker in the 22nd stitch to mark the center of the face.

12: sc 2, inc, (sc 5, inc) x 5, sc 3	(42)
13: (sc 6, inc) x 6	(48)
14: sc 19, inc, sc 7, inc, sc 20	(50)
15: sc 21, inc, sc 5, inc, sc 22	(52)
16: (sc 25, inc) x 2	(54)
17: sc 23, inc, sc 4, inc, sc 25	(56)

Attach safety eyes between rows 12 and 13, leaving 14 stitches (count 13 holes) between them (see page 7).

Add a bit of stuffing to the muzzle and embroider the nose (see page 7 - 8).

18-25: sc in each st	(56)
26: sc 5, dec, (sc 12, dec) x 3, sc 7	(52)
27: (sc 11, dec) x 4	(48)
28: sc 4, dec, (sc 10, dec) x 3, sc 6	(44)

Start stuffing the head. Keep adding a bit of fiberfill after every few rounds, stuffing the head firmly.

29: (sc 9, dec) x 4	(40)
30: sc 3, dec, (sc 8, dec) x 3, sc 5	(36)
31: (sc 7, dec) x 4	(32)
32: sc 2, dec, (sc 6, dec) x 3, sc 4	(28)
33: (sc 5, dec) x 4	(24)
34: (dec, sc 2) x 6	(18)
35: (sc, dec) x 6	(12)
36: dec x 6	(6)

Finish stuffing the head. Cut the yarn, leaving a long yarn tail, and fasten off. Pick up all the remaining stitches and close the opening (see page 8).

Ears (make 2)

With beige yarn:

1: mr, sc 6	(6)
2: (inc, sc) x 3	(9)
3: (sc 2, inc) x 3	(12)
4: sc, inc, (sc 3, inc) x 2, sc 2	(15)
5: (sc 4, inc) x 3	(18)
6: sc 2, inc, (sc 5, inc) x 2, sc 3	(21)
7: (sc 6, inc) x 3	(24)
8: (sc 11, inc) x 2	(26)
9: sc 5, inc, sc 12, inc, sc 7	(28)
10-15: sc in each st	(28)
16: (dec, sc 12) x 2	(26)
17: (dec, sc 11) x 2	(24)
18: (dec, sc 4) x 4	(20)

Sl st in next. Cut the yarn, leaving a long yarn tail for sewing, and fasten off. Do not stuff the ears.

Antlers (make 2)

Make the three tines first and then join them as you go (see page 9 - 10).

Tine 1

With white yarn:

1: mr, sc 6	(6)
2-4: sc in each st	(6)
5: sc 3, inc, sc 2	(7)
6: sc in each st	(7)
7: sc 4, inc, sc 2	(8)
8: sc in each st	(8)
9: sc 4, leave rest of the sts unworked	(8)

Sl st in next stitch and fasten off. Stuff firmly.

Tine 2

With white yarn:

1: mr, sc 6	(6)
2-3: sc in each st	(6)
...	

...

4: sc 3, inc, sc 2	(7)
5: sc in each st	(7)
6: sc 4, inc, sc 2	(8)
7-8: sc in each st	(8)
9: sc 4, leave rest of the sts unworked	(8)

Sl st in next stitch and fasten off. Stuff firmly.

Tine 3

With white yarn:

1: mr, sc 6	(6)
2-3: sc in each st	(6)
4: sc 3, inc, sc 2	(7)
5-6: sc in each st	(7)

Do not fasten off, leave the working yarn attached to the third tine. Stuff firmly.

Antler

With white yarn:

1: continue around the third tine: sc, take the second tine and continue around it, starting in the next stitch after the sl st: sc 8, continue around the third tine, starting in the next stitch: sc 2, dec, sc 2	(14)
2: dec, sc 6, dec, sc 4	(12)
3: (dec, sc 4) x 2	(10)
4: sc in each st	(10)

Start stuffing the antler. Keep adding a bit of fiberfill after every few rounds, stuffing the antler firmly.

5: sc 7, dec, sc	(9)
6-7: sc in each st	(9)
8: sc 4, take the first tine and continue around it, starting in the next stitch after the sl st: sc 8, continue around the antler, starting in the next stitch: sc 5	(17)
9: sc 3, dec, sc 6, dec, sc 4	(15)
10: sc, dec x 2, sc 3, dec x 2, sc 3	(11)
11-12: sc in each st	(11)
13: dec, sc 9	(10)

...

14-18: sc in each st	(10)

Sl st in next stitch. Cut the yarn, leaving a long yarn tail for sewing, and fasten off. Stuff firmly.

Arms (make 2)

With brown yarn:

1: mr, sc 6	(6)
2: inc x 6	(12)
3: (sc, inc) x 6	(18)
4: (inc, sc 2) x 6	(24)

Crochet round 5 in back loops only.

5: sc in each st	(24)
6: sc 7, dec, (sc 2, dec) x 2, sc 7	(21)
7: sc 8, dec, sc, dec, sc 8	(19)
8: (sc 5, dec) x 2, sc 5	(17)
9: dec, sc 6, dec, sc 7	(15)

Stuff firmly. Make a long vertical stitch along the front of the hoof and draw it tight (see page 10 - 11).

Keep adding a bit of fiberfill after every few rounds, stuffing the arms firmly.

With beige yarn:

10: sc 7, dec, sc 6	(14)
11: sc in each st	(14)
12: sc 7, dec, sc 5	(13)
13-14: sc in each st	(13)
15: sc 7, dec, sc 4	(12)
16-17: sc in each st	(12)
18: sc 7, dec, sc 3	(11)
19-30: sc in each st	(11)

On the left arm only, sc in next 6 stitches. Count the last stitch as the end of the round from now on.

Attach the joint between rows 29 and 30, placing it so the stem is facing straight towards the body (see page 11).

31: sc, dec x 5	(6)

Finish stuffing the arms. Cut the yarn, leaving a long yarn tail, and fasten off. Pick up all the remaining stitches and close the opening (see page 8).

Legs (make 2)

With brown yarn:

1: mr, sc 6 (6)
2: inc x 6 (12)
3: (sc, inc) x 6 (18)
4: (inc, sc 2) x 6 (24)
5: (sc 3, inc) x 6 (30)

Crochet round 6 in back loops only.

6: sc in each st (30)
7: sc 8, dec, (sc 2, dec) x 3, sc 8 (26)
8: sc 9, dec, (sc, dec) x 2, sc 9 (23)
9: sc 5, dec, sc 9, dec, sc 5 (21)
10: dec, sc 8, dec, sc 9 (19)

Stuff firmly. Make a long vertical stitch along the front of the hoof and draw it tight (see page 10 - 11).

Keep adding a bit of fiberfill after every few rounds, stuffing the legs firmly.

With beige yarn:

11: sc 6, dec, sc 3, dec, sc 6 (17)
12: sc 8, dec, sc 7 (16)
13: sc in each st (16)
14: sc 8, dec, sc 6 (15)
15-16: sc in each st (15)
17: sc 8, dec, sc 5 (14)
18-32: sc in each st (14)

On the left leg only, *sc* in next 7 stitches. Count the last stitch as the end of the round from now on.

Attach the joint between rows 31 and 32, placing it so the stem is facing towards the body (see page 11).

33: sc 2, dec, sc 7, dec, sc (12)
34: dec x 6 (6)

Finish stuffing the legs. Cut the yarn, leaving a long yarn tail, and fasten off. Pick up all the remaining stitches and close the opening (see page 8).

Body

With beige yarn:

1: mr, sc 6 (6)
2: inc x 6 (12)
...
3: (sc, inc) x 6 (18)
4: (inc, sc 2) x 6 (24)
5: (sc 3, inc) x 6 (30)
6: sc, inc, (sc 4, inc) x 5, sc 3 (36)
7: sc 3, inc, (sc 8, inc) x 3, sc 5 (40)
8: (sc 9, inc) x 4 (44)
9-16: sc in each st (44)

Turn the body so the end of the round is at the center of the back. Attach the legs to the sides of the body, between rounds 9 and 10 (see page 12).

17: (sc 9, dec) x 4 (40)
18: sc 3, dec, (sc 8, dec) x 3, sc 5 (36)
19: (sc 7, dec) x 4 (32)
20: sc in each st (32)
21: (dec, sc 14) x 2 (30)

Start stuffing the body. Keep adding a bit of fiberfill after every few rounds, stuffing the body firmly.

22: sc in each st (30)
23: sc 12, dec, sc 4, dec, sc 10 (28)
24: sc in each st (28)
25: (dec, sc 5) x 4 (24)
26: sc in each st (24)
27: sc 9, dec, sc 4, dec, sc 7 (22)
28: sc in each st (22)
29: sc 5, dec, sc 9, dec, sc 4 (20)
30-33: sc in each st (20)
34: sc 5, leave rest of the sts unworked (20)

Sl st in next stitch. Cut the yarn, leaving a long yarn tail for sewing, and fasten off.

Attach the arms to the sides of the body, between rounds 29 and 30 (see page 12). Finish stuffing.

Tail

With beige yarn:

1: mr, sc 6 (6)
2: (sc 2, inc) x 2 (8)
3: sc, inc, sc 3, inc, sc 2 (10)
4: sc in each st (10)
5: (dec, sc 3) x 2 (8)

Sl st in next stitch. Cut the yarn, leaving a long yarn tail for sewing, and fasten off. Do not stuff the tail.

Head

a) Attach safety eyes after finishing round 17.

1. Place the eyes to either side of the stitch marker, between rows 12 and 13, leaving 14 stitches (count 13 holes) between them.

2. Make sure you are satisfied with the placement of the eyes before pushing the washer into place.

b) Embroider the nose.

1. Add a bit of stuffing to the muzzle. Insert the needle from inside the head and bring it up just above the first round.

2. Make a few stitches to mark the shape and size of the nose.

3. Just keep stitching, trying to keep even tension ...

4. ... and fill in all the gaps.

5. Make a long stitch across the top of the nose to hide any imperfections.

6. Knot the yarn ends together inside the head.

c) Finish the head and close the opening.

1. Cut the yarn, leaving a long tail, and fasten off. Thread the yarn tail onto a yarn needle.

2. Pick up all the remaining stitches onto the yarn, inserting the needle from the center and under the front loop only and draw the yarn through.

3. Grab the yarn tail and pull until the hole is tightly closed.

4. Insert the needle through the center and bring the yarn to the side of the head. Fasten and hide the yarn tail.

d) Use yarn to shape the head.

1. Insert the needle from the bottom of the head, between rounds 16 and 18, and bring it up right next to the eye.

2. Go about half way around the eye and insert the needle right next to the eye. Bring it to the bottom of the head.

3. Grab the yarn tails and tug gently, pulling the eye in just a bit.

4. Knot the yarn tails together. Do the same with the other eye.

Antlers

a) Make the three tines first and then join them as you go.

1. Take the third tine and continue around it, crocheting one *sc* in next stitch.

2. Take the second tine and continue around it, starting in the next stitch after the slip stitch.

3. Go around the second tine, crocheting one *sc* in each stitch.

4. Continue around the third tine, starting in the next stitch.

5. Go around the third tine: *sc* 2, *dec*, *sc* 2. Continue crocheting in spiral.

6. Join the first tine the same way.

Arms & Legs

a) Make a long stitch along the front of the hoofs.

1. Finish the hoof and stuff it firmly. Insert the needle from the top, leaving a short yarn tail, and bring it up between the last two rounds.

2. Go straight down and insert the needle just above the first round.

3. Come back out through the opening. Grab the yarn tails and draw the stitch very tight.

4. Knot the yarn ends together.

b) Place the disk with a stem or a button inside the arms and legs.

1. Place the disk inside the limb so the stem is facing straight towards the body.

2. Finish the arms and legs and close the opening (see page 8).

Assembling the deer

a) Sew the ears to the head.

Tip! Sew the ears and antlers to the head before you sew the head to the body - this way you can fasten all yarn tails securely with a knot under the head.

1. Place the ears just behind round 21 of the head, leaving 21 – 22 stitches between them.

2. Flatten the ear and start sewing it to the head.

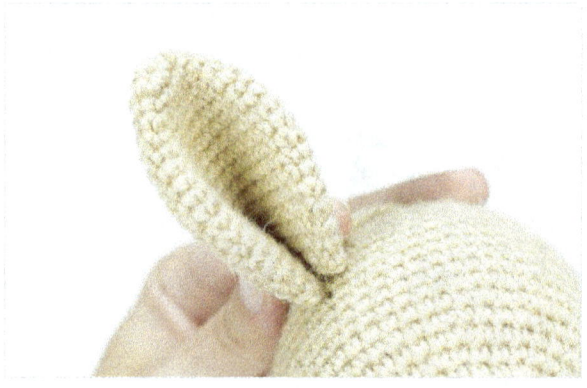

3. When you reach the center, fold the ear in half.

4. And sew the second side right next to the first.

b) Sew the antlers to the head.

1. Place the antlers just behind round 21 of the head, leaving 10 – 11 stitches between them.

2. Sew the antlers to the head (see page 16).

c) Finish the arms and legs. Start making the body and attach the limbs as you go.

1. Turn the body so the end of the round is at the center of the back. Attach the legs to either side of the body between rounds 9 and 10.

2. Finish the body. Attach the arms to either side of the body between rounds 29 and 30.

d) Sew the head to the body.

1. Sew the head to the body (see page 16), placing it so the front edge is just behind round 15 of the head.

2. Add a bit more stuffing before closing the seam.

e) Sew the tail to the body.

1. Flatten the tail and place it over the 8th round of the body.

2. Sew the tail to the body.

Reindeer

Crochet pattern by Kristi Tullus

Size

About 30.5 cm (12") tall, including antlers, when crocheted with sport weight cotton and acrylic blend and a 2.50 mm hook.

Skills required

Crocheting in spiral, chain, slip and single crochet stitch, increasing and decreasing.

Difficulty

3. Intermediate – includes some less common crochet techniques and color changes.

Contact Info

Pattern includes unlimited support from me over email (kristi@spire.ee). Photo and video tutorials and tips are available on my website https://kristitullus.com

Copyright © 2020 TÜ Spire. Contents of this document MAY NOT be copied, reproduced, altered, published or distributed in any way. You MAY sell finished products made with this pattern, I would appreciate a credit as the designer (Kristi Tullus, kristitullus.com).

Tip! You can use the same pattern to make larger or smaller toys by using finer or bulkier yarn. Make sure to pick a crochet hook at least a size smaller than suggested on the yarn label and crochet tightly enough to achieve a tight gauge that will not allow the stuffing to show through the fabric. You may also need to adjust the size of the safety eyes and joints.

Materials & Tools

- Yarn. I used Scheepjes *Stone Washed*, a sport weight cotton-acrylic blend, 50 g = 130 m (50 g = 142 yd). You will need about 55 g of beige and 20 g of brown yarn. And Alize *Cotton Gold*, a sport weight cotton-acrylic blend, 100 g = 330 m (100 g = 361 yd). You will need about 8 g of blue and 2 g of white yarn.
- 2.50 – 3.00 mm crochet hook (US size 2/C - 3/D) or according to the yarn.
- Polyester fiberfill, wool, wadding etc. for stuffing.
- 12 mm (1/2") safety eyes or buttons, beads, felt etc.
- Two 20 mm (4/5") and two 15 mm (3/5") doll joints or safety eyes or buttons.
- Black or dark brown cotton embroidery floss.
- Yarn needle, scissors, stitch marker.

Choosing joints

Tip! You can use plastic doll joints, safety eyes, cotter pin joints, buttons and thread or even just thread to attach the arms and legs. My favorite are plastic doll joints - they are easy to install, durable and washable. Buttons and thread will work great as well, if you can't get your hands on any joints.

Plastic doll joints

1. Plastic doll joints come in three pieces - disk with a post, washer and a fastener.

2. Disk with a post is placed inside the limbs, pushing the post through the fabric.

3. And then locked in place inside the body.

Button and thread joints

Tip! Make sure you use very strong thread to attach the limbs – it will have to endure quite a bit of tension and can be a bit difficult to mend, should it break. I have found cotton embroidery floss, nylon sewing thread (doubled or tripled) or fishing line work really well.

1. Cut a length of yarn and draw it through the holes in the button.

2. Place the button inside a limb, drawing the yarn tails through the fabric.

3. Place the other button inside the body, draw the yarn tails through the holes and knot them together.

Abbreviations

- **st(s)** = stitch(es).
- **mr, sc** *n* = crochet *n* (number) single crochet stitches in to the adjustable loop (see page 16).
- **ch** = chain stitch.
- **sl st** = slip stitch (single crochet stitch in UK and Australia).
- **sc** = single crochet stitch (double crochet stitch in UK and Australia).
- **dc** = double crochet stitch (triple or treble crochet stitch in UK and Australia).
- **bpsc** = back post single crochet stitch (see page 15).
- **sc (or sl st, ch etc.)** *n* = crochet *n* single crochet stitches (or sl st, ch etc.), one in each stitch.
- **inc** = increase – crochet two single crochet stitches in the same stitch.
- **inc3** = double increase – crochet three single crochet stitches in the same stitch.
- **dec** = decrease – crochet two stitches together using the invisible decrease method (see page 17-18).
- **(sc 4, inc) x** *n* = repeat the pattern between parentheses *n* times.
- **(36)** = number of stitches in a round after finishing round.

Notes

- Work in a continuous spiral, do not join rounds or turn your work, unless instructed otherwise in the pattern.
- Use a stitch marker or a piece of yarn to mark the end or the beginning of a round. Move the marker up after completing each round.
- Work all stitches in both loops, unless instructed otherwise in the pattern.
- Make sure to crochet tightly enough to achieve a tight gauge that will not allow the stuffing to show through the fabric.

Head

With beige yarn:

1: mr, sc 6	(6)
2: inc x 6	(12)
3: (sc, inc) x 6	(18)
4: (inc, sc 2) x 6	(24)
5: (sc 7, inc) x 3	(27)
6: sc in each st	(27)
7: sc 3, inc, (sc 8, inc) x 2, sc 5	(30)
8: sc in each st	(30)
9: (sc 9, inc) x 3	(33)
10: sc in each st	(33)
11: sc 4, inc, (sc 10, inc) x 2, sc 6	(36)
12: sc 2, inc, (sc 5, inc) x 5, sc 3	(42)

On round 13, place a stitch marker between stitches 23 and 24 (around the loops on top of the 24th stitch) to mark the center of the face. Use it as guide when placing the eyes.

13: (sc 6, inc) x 6	(48)
14: sc 18, inc, sc 8, inc, sc 20	(50)
15: sc 21, inc, sc 5, inc, sc 22	(52)
16: (sc 25, inc) x 2	(54)
17: sc 23, inc, sc 4, inc, sc 25	(56)

Attach safety eyes to either side of the stitch marker, between rounds 13 and 14, leaving 16 stitches (count 15 holes) between them (see page 7).

18-24: sc in each st	(56)
25: (sc 12, dec) x 4	(52)
26: sc 5, dec, (sc 11, dec) x 3, sc 6	(48)
27: (sc 10, dec) x 4	(44)

Start stuffing the head. Keep adding a bit of fiberfill after every few rounds, stuffing the head firmly.

28: sc 4, dec, (sc 9, dec) x 3, sc 5	(40)
29: (sc 8, dec) x 4	(36)
30: sc, dec, (sc 4, dec) x 5, sc 3	(30)
31: (sc 3, dec) x 6	(24)
32: (dec, sc 2) x 6	(18)
33: (sc, dec) x 6	(12)
34: dec x 6	(6)

Finish stuffing the head. Cut the yarn, leaving a long yarn tail, and fasten off. Thread the tail onto a needle and use it to pick up all the remaining stitches and close the opening (see page 7). Use yarn to shape the head (see page 8).

Nose

With brown yarn:

1: mr, sc 6	(6)
2: (inc3 x 2, sc) x 2	(14)
3: sc in each st	(14)

Sl st in next stitch. Cut the yarn, leaving a long yarn tail for sewing, and fasten off. Stuff the nose firmly.

Ears (make 2)

With beige yarn:

1: mr, sc 6	(6)
2: sc in each st	(6)
3: (inc, sc) x 3	(9)
4: (sc 2, inc) x 3	(12)
5: sc, inc, (sc 3, inc) x 2, sc 2	(15)
6: (sc 4, inc) x 3	(18)
7-9: sc in each st	(18)
10: sc 3, dec, sc 7, dec, sc 4	(16)
11: sc in each st	(16)

Sl st in next stitch. Cut the yarn, leaving a long yarn tail for sewing, and fasten off. Do not stuff the ears.

Antlers (make 2)

Finish the two tines first and then join them as you go (see page 9).

Tine 1

With brown yarn:

1: mr, sc 6	(6)
2-5: sc in each st	(6)

Sl st in next stitch. Cut the yarn, fasten off and hide the yarn tail (see page 18). Stuff firmly.

Tine 2

With brown yarn:

1: mr, sc 6	(6)
2-7: sc in each st	(6)

Do not fasten off, leave the working yarn attached to the second tine. Stuff firmly.

Antler

With brown yarn:

1: continue around the second tine and sc in next st, take the first tine and continue around it, starting in the next stitch after the *sl st*: sc 2, dec, sc 2, continue around the second tine, starting in the next stitch: sc 2, dec, sc (10)
2: sc in each st (10)
3: (dec, sc 3) x 2 (8)
4-5: sc in each st (8)
6: sc 3, leave the rest of the sts unworked (8)

Sl st in next stitch. Cut the yarn, leaving a long yarn tail for sewing, and fasten off. Stuff the antlers firmly.

Arms (make 2)

With brown yarn:

1: mr, sc 6 (6)
2: inc x 6 (12)
3: (sc, inc) x 6 (18)
4: (inc, sc 2) x 6 (24)
5: bpsc in each st (24)
6: sc 7, dec, (sc 2, dec) x 2, sc 7 (21)
7: sc 8, dec, sc, dec, sc 8 (19)
8: (sc 5, dec) x 2, sc 5 (17)

Keep adding a bit of fiberfill after every few rounds, stuffing the arms firmly.

With beige yarn:

9: dec, sc 6, dec, sc 7 (15)

Stuff firmly. Make a long vertical stitch along the front of the hoof and draw it tight (see page 10).

10: sc in each st (15)
11: sc 7, dec, sc 6 (14)
12: sc in each st (14)
13: sc 7, dec, sc 5 (13)
14-15: sc in each st (13)
16: sc 7, dec, sc 4 (12)
17-26: sc in each st (12)

On the left arm only, *sc* in next 6 stitches. Count the last stitch as the end of the round from now on.

…

Attach the joint between rounds 25 and 26, placing it so the post is facing straight towards the body (see page 10).

27: sc 4, dec x 4 (8)
28: dec x 2, leave the rest of the sts unworked (6)

Finish stuffing the arms. Cut the yarn, leaving a long yarn tail, and fasten off. Thread the tail onto a needle and use it to pick up all the remaining stitches and close the opening (see page 7).

Legs (make 2)

With brown yarn:

1: mr, sc 6 (6)
2: inc x 6 (12)
3: (sc, inc) x 6 (18)
4: (inc, sc 2) x 6 (24)
5: (sc 3, inc) x 6 (30)
6: bpsc in each st (30)
7: sc 8, dec, (sc 4, dec) x 2, sc 8 (27)
8: sc 10, dec, sc 3, dec, sc 10 (25)
9: sc 6, dec, sc 10, dec, sc 5 (23)

Keep adding a bit of fiberfill after every few rounds, stuffing the legs firmly.

With beige yarn:

10: dec, sc 9, dec, sc 10 (21)

Stuff firmly. Make a long vertical stitch along the front of the hoof and draw it tight (see page 10).

11: sc 7, dec, sc 4, dec, sc 6 (19)
12: sc 9, dec, sc 8 (18)
13: sc in each st (18)
14: (dec, sc 7) x 2 (16)
15: sc in each st (16)
16: sc 8, dec, sc 6 (15)
17-18: sc in each st (15)
19: sc 8, dec, sc 5 (14)
20-31: sc in each st (14)

On the left leg only, *sc* in next 7 stitches. Count the last stitch as the end of the round from now on.

Attach the joint between rows 30 and 31, placing it so the post is facing towards the body (see page 10).

…

...

32: sc 2, dec, sc 7, dec, sc (12)
33: dec x 6 (6)

Finish stuffing the legs. Cut the yarn, leaving a long yarn tail, and fasten off. Thread the tail onto a needle and use it to pick up all the remaining stitches and close the opening (see page 7).

Body

With beige yarn:

1: mr, sc 6 (6)
2: inc x 6 (12)
3: (sc, inc) x 6 (18)
4: (inc, sc 2) x 6 (24)
5: (sc 3, inc) x 6 (30)
6: sc, inc, (sc 4, inc) x 5, sc 3 (36)
7: (sc 5, inc) x 6 (42)
8-14: sc in each st (42)

Turn the body so the last stitch of round 14 is facing away from you (center of the back). Attach the legs to the sides of the body, between rounds 8 and 9 (see page 11).

15: sc 10, dec, (sc 8, dec) x 2, sc 10 (39)
16: sc 14, dec, 7, dec, sc 14 (37)
17: sc 18, dec, sc 17 (36)
18: (dec, sc 10) x 3 (33)
19: sc in each st (33)

Start stuffing the body. Keep adding a bit of fiberfill after every few rounds, stuffing the body firmly.

20: sc 5, dec, (sc 9, dec) x 2, sc 4 (30)
21: sc in each st (30)
22: (dec, sc 8) x 3 (27)
23: sc in each st (27)
24: sc 4, dec, (sc 7, dec) x 2, sc 3 (24)
25: sc in each st (24)
26: (dec, sc 6) x 3 (21)
27: sc in each st (21)
28: sc 10, dec, sc 9 (20)
29: sc 6, leave the rest of the sts unworked (20)

Sl st in next stitch. Cut the yarn, leaving a long yarn tail for sewing, and fasten off.

Attach arms to the sides of the body, between rounds 24 and 25 (see page 11). Finish stuffing the body.

Tail

With beige yarn:

1: mr, sc 6 (6)
2: (sc 2, inc) x 2 (8)
3: sc, inc, sc 3, inc, sc 2 (10)
4: (sc 4, inc) x 2 (12)
5: sc in each st (12)
6: (dec, sc) x 4 (8)

Sl st in next stitch. Cut the yarn, leaving a long yarn tail for sewing, and fasten off. Stuff the tail lightly.

Scarf

With blue yarn:

1: ch 52. Starting in 3rd ch from hook, dc in each ch, crocheted into back "bumps" Ch 2, sl st in 1st ch (see page 14). (50)

Fasten off and weave in the yarn tails.

Hat

With white yarn:

1: mr, sc 6 (6)
2: inc x 6 (12)
3-4: sc in each st (12)
5: dec x 6 (6)

Stuff firmly.

With blue yarn:

6: sc in each st (6)
7: (inc, sc) x 3 (9)
8: sc in each st (9)
9: (sc 2, inc) x 3 (12)
10: sc in each st (12)
11: sc, inc, (sc 3, inc) x 2, sc 2 (15)
12-17: sc in each st (15)
18: (sc 4, inc) x 3 (18)
19: sc in each st (18)
20: sc 2, inc, (sc 5, inc) x 2, sc 3 (21)
21: sc in each st (21)
22: (sc 6, inc) x 3 (24)
23: sc in each st (24)
24: sc 3, inc, (sc 7, inc) x 2, sc 4 (27)

Sl st in next stitch. Cut the yarn, leaving a long yarn tail for sewing, and fasten off. Fold down the tip of the hat (see page 13). Stuff the hat lightly.

Head

a) Attach safety eyes after finishing round 17.

1. Place the eyes to either side of the stitch marker, between rounds 13 and 14, leaving 16 stitches (count 15 holes) between them.

2. Make sure you are satisfied with the placement of the eyes before pushing the washer into place.

b) Finish the head and close the opening.

1. Cut the yarn, leaving a long tail, and fasten off. Thread the yarn tail onto a yarn needle.

2. Pick up all the remaining stitches onto the yarn. Insert the needle from the center and under the front loop only and draw the yarn through.

3. Grab the yarn tail and pull until the hole is tightly closed.

4. Insert the needle through the center and bring the yarn to the bottom of the head.

c) Use yarn to shape the head.

1. Insert the needle from the bottom of the head, between rounds 15 and 16, and bring it up right next to the eye.

2. Insert the needle on the other side of the eye and go through the head towards the other eye.

2. Bring the needle up right next to the other eye.

4. Insert the needle on the other side of the eye and come back out at the bottom of the head.

5. Grab the yarn tails and tug gently, pulling the eyes in just a bit.

6. Knot the yarn tails together.

Antlers

a) Make the two tines first and then join them as you go.

1. Take the second tine and crochet one *sc* in next stitch. Then take the first tine and continue around it, starting in the next stitch after the slip stitch.

2. Insert your hook in that stitch and complete a *sc* as you would normally.

3. Go around the first tine and crochet *sc 2, dec, sc 2*.

4. Continue around the second tine, starting in the next stitch.

5. Go around the second tine and crochet *sc 2, dec, sc*.

6. And now you should have 10 stitches in the round. Continue crocheting in spiral.

Arms & Legs

a) Make a long stitch along the front of the hoof.

1. Finish the hoof and stuff it firmly. Insert the needle from the top, leaving a short yarn tail, and bring it up just above the last round you crocheted with brown yarn.

2. Go straight down and insert the needle just above the first round.

3. Come back out through the opening. Grab the yarn tails and draw the stitch very tight.

4. Knot the yarn ends together.

b) Place the joint or a button inside the arms and legs.

1. Place the disk inside the limb so the post is facing straight towards the body.

2. Finish the arms and legs and close the opening (see page 7).

Body

a) Finish the arms and legs. Start making the body and attach the limbs as you go.

1. Turn the body so the end of the round is at the center of the back. Attach the legs to the sides of the body between rounds 8 and 9.

2. Finish the body. Attach the arms to the sides of the body between rounds 24 and 25.

Assembling the Reindeer

a) Sew the nose to the head.

1. Place the nose just above round 2 of the head.

2. Sew the nose to the head with whip stitch.

b) Sew the antlers to the head.

1. Place the antlers just behind round 20, leaving 12 - 13 stitches between them.

2. Sew the antlers to the head with whip stitch.

c) Sew the ears to the head.

1. Flatten the ears and fold them in half lengthwise.

2. Place the ears just behind round 20, one stitch below the antlers.

3. Start sewing the ear to the head.

4. When you reach the center, fold the ear in half and sew the second side right next to the first one.

Tip! Sew the nose, antlers and ears to the head and add any embellishments before you sew the head to the body - this way you can fasten all yarn tails securely with a knot under the head.

d) Sew the tail to the body.

1. Flatten the tail a little.

2. Sew the tail over round 8 with whip or mattress stitch.

e) Sew the head to the body.

1. Sew the head to the body with whip stitch, placing it so the front edge of the body is just behind round 13 of the head.

2. Add a bit more stuffing before closing the seam.

Hat

a) Finish the hat and fold down the tip. Sew the hat to the head.

1. Cut a length of yarn and thread it onto a needle. Fold down the tip of the hat. Insert the needle from inside the hat, leaving a short yarn tail.

2. Make a little stitch and come back out on the inside of the hat.

3. Knot the yarn ends together. Stuff the hat lightly.

4. Sew the hat to the head with whip stitch.

Scarf

Tip! The edge of the scarf will look nicer, if you crochet all stitches into the "bumps" on the back of the starting chain.

1. Flip the chain over and insert your hook under the loop or "bump" on the back of each chain stitch.

2. This will leave a nice neat row of loops along the bottom edge.

3. *Dc* in each *ch*. Then *ch 2* and *sl st* in the first *ch* of the starting chain. Fasten off and weave in the yarn tails.

4. Tie the scarf around the reindeer's neck.

Raccoon

CROCHET PATTERN BY KRISTI TULLUS

SIZE

25 cm (10") from head to toe, when crocheted with sport weight cotton-acrylic blend and a 2,50 mm hook.

SKILLS REQUIRED

Crocheting in spiral, chain, slip and single crochet stitch, increasing and decreasing.

DIFFICULTY

3. Intermediate – includes some less common crochet techniques, color changes and simple shaping.

MATERIALS & TOOLS

- Yarn. I used Scheepjes 'Stone Washed', a sport weight cotton and acrylic blend, 130 m = 50 g (142 yd = 50 g) / 12 wpi / 2: fine. You will need about 70 g of light gray (802 smokey quartz), 17 g of dark gray (803 black onyx) and 7 g of white yarn (801 moon stone).
- 2,50 - 3,50 mm crochet hook (US size 2/C - 4/E) or according to the yarn.
- Polyester fiberfill, wool, wadding for stuffing.
- 9 mm (1/3") safety eyes and a 12 mm (1/2") triangular safety nose or buttons, beads, felt etc.
- Two 20 mm (4/5") and two 15 mm (3/5") doll joints or safety eyes or buttons and thread.
- Black cotton embroidery floss.
- Yarn needle, scissors, stitch marker.

CHOOSING JOINTS

Tip! You can use plastic doll joints, cotter pin joints, buttons and thread or even just thread to attach the arms and legs. My favorite are plastic doll joints - they are easy to install, durable and washable. Buttons and thread will work great as well, if you can't get your hands on any joints.

Plastic doll joints

1. Plastic doll joints come in three pieces - disk with a stem, washer and a fastener.

2. Disk with a stem is placed inside the limbs, pushing the stem through the fabric.

3. And then locked to place inside the body.

Button and thread joints

Tip! Make sure you use a very strong thread to attach the limbs – it will have to endure quite a bit of tension and can be a bit difficult to mend, should it break. I have found cotton embroidery floss, nylon sewing thread (doubled or tripled) or fishing line work really well.

1. Cut a length of yarn and draw it through the holes in the button.

2. Place the button inside a limb, drawing the yarn tails through the fabric.

3. Place the other button inside the body, draw the yarn tails through the holes and knot them together.

ABBREVIATIONS

- **st(s)** = stitch(es).
- **mr, sc** *n* = magic ring - start with an adjustable loop and crochet *n* (number) single crochet stitches into the adjustable loop (see page 13).
- **ch** = chain stitch.
- **sl st** = slip stitch (single crochet stitch in UK and Australia).
- **sc** = single crochet stitch (double crochet stitch in UK and Australia).
- **sc (or sl st, ch, hdc etc.)** *n* = make *n* single crochet stitches (or sl st, ch, hdc etc.), one in each stitch.
- **sc + sl st** = crochet sc and then sl st in the same stitch.
- **inc** = increase – crochet two single crochet stitches in the same stitch.
- **inc3** = double increase – crochet three single crochet stitches in the same stitch.
- **dec** = decrease – crochet two stitches together using the invisible decrease method (see page 15).
- **(sc 4, inc) x** *n* = repeat the pattern between parentheses *n* times.
- **(36)** = number of stitches in a round after finishing round.

NOTES

- Work in a continuous spiral, do not join rounds or turn your work, unless instructed otherwise in the pattern.
- Use a stitch marker or a piece of yarn to mark the end or the beginning of a round.
- Work all stitches in both loops, unless instructed otherwise in the pattern.

COPYRIGHT INFO

Copyright © 2019 Kristi Tullus, TÜ Spire. All rights reserved. Contents of this document may not be copied, reproduced, altered, published or distributed in any way. Feel free to sell finished products made with this pattern, I would appreciate a credit as the designer (Kristi Tullus, kristitullus.com).

HEAD

With light gray yarn:

1: mr, sc 6	(6)
2: inc x 6	(12)
3: (sc, inc) x 6	(18)
4: (inc, sc 2) x 6	(24)
5: (sc 3, inc) x 6	(30)
6: sc, inc, (sc 4, inc) x 5, sc 3	(36)
7: (sc 5, inc) x 6	(42)
8: sc 2, inc, (sc 6, inc) x 5, sc 4	(48)
9-10: sc in each st	(48)
11: sc 5, inc, (sc 11, inc) x 3, sc 6	(52)
12: sc 22, with dark gray yarn: sc 2, with light gray yarn: sc 3, with dark gray yarn: sc 2, with light gray yarn: sc 23	(52)
13: sc 12, inc, sc 8, with dark gray yarn: sc 4, with light gray yarn: inc, sc, with dark gray yarn: sc 4, with light gray yarn: sc 7, inc, sc 12, inc	(56)
14: sc 21, with dark gray yarn: sc 5, with light gray yarn: sc 3, with dark gray yarn: sc 5, with light gray yarn: sc 22	(56)
15: sc 9, inc, sc 7, inc, sc 2, with dark gray yarn: sc 6, with light gray yarn: sc 3, with dark gray yarn: sc 6, with light gray yarn: sc 2, inc, sc 7, inc, sc 10	(60)
16: sc 21, with dark gray yarn: sc 7, with light gray yarn: sc 3, with dark gray yarn: sc 7, with light gray yarn: sc 22	(60)
17-19: sc 21, with dark gray yarn: sc 18, with light gray yarn: sc 21	(60)
20: sc 22, with dark gray yarn: sc 17, with with light gray yarn: sc 21	(60)
21: sc 23, with dark gray yarn: sc 16, with with light gray yarn: sc 21	(60)
22: sc 3, (dec, sc 8) x 2, with dark gray yarn: dec, sc 8, dec, sc 3, with light gray yarn: sc 5, dec, sc 8, dec, sc 5	(54)
23: (sc 7, dec) x 2, sc 4, with dark gray yarn: sc 3, dec, sc 6, with light gray yarn: sc, dec, (sc 7, dec) x 2	(48)

Attach safety eyes between rounds 16 and 17, leaving 11 stitches (count 10 holes) between them (see page 7).

...

Embroider the "eyebrows" (see page 7).

24: sc 2, dec, (sc 6, dec) x 5, sc 4	(42)
25: (sc 5, dec) x 6	(36)

Start stuffing the head. Keep adding a bit of fiberfill after every few rounds, stuffing the head firmly.

26: sc, dec, (sc 4, dec) x 5, sc 3	(30)
27: (sc 3, dec) x 6	(24)
28: (dec, sc 2) x 6	(18)

Sl st in next stitch. Cut the yarn, leaving a long yarn tail for sewing, and fasten off. Stuff the head firmly.

MUZZLE

With white yarn:

1: mr, sc 6	(6)
2: inc x 6	(12)
3: (sc, inc x 2) x 4	(20)
4: sc in each st	(20)
5: (sc 3, inc) x 5	(25)
6: sc in each st	(25)
7: sc, inc, (sc 4, inc) x 4, sc 3	(30)

Sl st in next stitch. Cut the yarn, leaving a long yarn tail for sewing, and fasten off. Add a nose and mouth (see page 8).

EARS (make 2)

Make one with light and one with dark gray yarn:

1: mr, sc 6	(6)
2: (sc, inc3) x 3	(12)
3: sc 2, inc3, (sc 3, inc3) x 2, sc	(18)

Sl st in next stitch and fasten off.

Align a light and dark gray piece, wrong sides facing. Crochet over the edge with single crochet stitches, following the instruction below, inserting the hook through both layers (see page 8). Locate the middle stitch of the first *inc3* and attach the white yarn with a *sl st*. Starting in the same stitch:

4: sc 6, inc3, sc 5, sc + sl st

Cut the yarn and fasten off. Hide the yarn tails inside the ears.

LEFT ARM

With dark gray yarn:

1: mr, sc 6	(6)
2: (inc3 x 2, sc) x 2	(14)
3-5: sc in each st	(14)
6: sc 3, inc, sc 5, dec x 2, sc	(13)
7: sc 4, inc, sc 5, dec, sc	(13)
8: sc 11, dec	(12)

Stuff the hands firmly. Keep adding a bit of fiberfill after every few rounds, stuffing the arms firmly.

Sc in next three stitches. Count the last sc as the end of the round from now on.

9: sc in each st	(12)
10: sc 8, dec, sc 2	(11)

With light gray yarn:

11-23: sc in each st	(11)

Attach the smaller joint between rounds 22 and 23, placing it so the stem is facing straight towards the body.

24: sc, dec x 5	(6)

Finish stuffing. Cut the yarn, leaving a long yarn tail, and fasten off. Pick up all the remaining stitches and close the opening (see page 9 - 10).

RIGHT ARM

With dark gray yarn:

1: mr, sc 6	(6)
2: (inc3 x 2, sc) x 2	(14)
3-5: sc in each st	(14)
6: sc 2, dec x 2, sc 5, inc, sc 2	(13)
7: sc 2, dec, sc 5, inc, sc 3	(13)
8: sc 2, dec, sc 9	(12)

Stuff the hands firmly. Keep adding a bit of fiberfill after every few rounds, stuffing the arms firmly.

9: sc in each st	(12)
10: sc 2, dec, sc 8	(11)

...

With light gray yarn:

11-23: sc in each st	(11)

Attach the smaller joint between rounds 22 and 23, placing it so the stem is facing straight towards the body.

24: sc, dec x 5	(6)

Finish stuffing. Cut the yarn, leaving a long yarn tail, and fasten off. Pick up all the remaining stitches and close the opening (see page 9 - 10).

LEGS (make 2)

With dark gray yarn:

1: mr, sc 6	(6)
2: inc x 6	(12)
3: (sc, inc) x 6	(18)
4: (sc 3, inc) x 4, sc 2	(22)
5: sc in each st	(22)
6: sc 8, dec, sc 2, dec, sc 8	(20)
7: sc 6, dec, (sc, dec) x 2, sc 6	(17)
8: sc 6, dec, sc 2, dec, sc 5	(15)
9: sc 7, dec, sc 6	(14)

Stuff the feet firmly. Keep adding a bit of fiberfill after every few rounds, stuffing the legs firmly.

10: sc in each st	(14)
11: sc 7, dec, sc 5	(13)
12-13: sc in each st	(13)

With light gray yarn:

14-26: sc in each st	(13)

On the right leg only, sc in next 6 stitches. Count the last sc as the end of the round from now on.

Attach the larger joint between rounds 25 and 26, placing it so the stem is facing straight towards the body.

27: sc 4, dec, sc 3, dec, sc 2	(11)
28: sc, dec x 5	(6)

Finish stuffing. Cut the yarn, leaving a long yarn tail, and fasten off. Pick up all the remaining stitches and close the opening (see page 9 - 10).

BODY

With light gray yarn:

1: mr, sc 6	(6)
2: inc x 6	(12)
3: (sc, inc) x 6	(18)
4: (inc, sc 2) x 6	(24)
5: (sc 3, inc) x 6	(30)
6: sc, inc, (sc 4, inc) x 5, sc 3	(36)
7: (sc 5, inc) x 6	(42)
8-14: sc in each st	(42)

Turn the body so the last stitch of round 14 is facing away from you (center of the back). Attach the legs to the sides of the body, between rounds 8 and 9 (see page 11).

15: sc 9, dec, sc 5, dec, sc 6, dec, sc 5, dec, sc 9	(38)
16: sc 11, dec, (sc 5, dec) x 2, sc 11	(35)
17: sc 4, dec, sc 24, dec, dc 3	(33)
18: (dec, sc 9) x 3	(30)

Start stuffing the body. Keep adding a bit of fiberfill after every few rounds, stuffing the body firmly.

19: sc in each st	(30)
20: sc 4, dec, (sc 8, dec) x 2, sc 4	(27)
21: sc in each st	(27)
22: (dec, sc 7) x 3	(24)
23: sc in each st	(24)
24: sc 3, dec, (sc 6, dec) x 2, sc 3	(21)
25: sc in each st	(21)
26: (dec, sc 5) x 3	(18)
27-28: sc in each st	(18)

Sl st in next stitch. Cut the yarn and fasten off.

Attach the arms to the sides of the body, between rounds 23 and 24 (see page 11). Finish stuffing the body.

TAIL

With dark gray yarn:

1: mr, 6	(6)
2: (sc, inc) x 3	(9)
3: (inc, sc 2) x 3	(12)

With light gray yarn:

4: (sc 2, inc) x 4	(16)
5-6: sc in each st	(16)

With dark gray yarn:

7-8: sc in each st	(16)

Sc in next stitch. Count the last sc as the end of the round from now on.

With light gray yarn:

9: sc in each st	(16)
10: (dec, sc 6) x 2	(14)
11: sc in each st	(14)

Start stuffing the tail. Keep adding a bit of fiberfill after every few rounds, stuffing the tail firmly.

With dark gray yarn:

12: sc in each st	(14)
13: sc 7, dec, sc 5	(13)

Sc in next stitch. Count the last sc as the end of the round from now on.

With light gray yarn:

14-15: sc in each st	(13)
16: sc 6, dec, sc 5	(12)

With dark gray yarn:

17-18: sc in each st	(12)

Sc in next stitch. Count the last sc as the end of the round from now on.

With light gray yarn:

19: sc 5, dec, sc 5	(11)
20: sc in each st	(11)
21: dec, sc 3, dec, sc 4	(9)

Sl st in next stitch. Cut the yarn, leaving a long yarn tail for sewing, and fasten off. Finish stuffing the tail.

Sew the muzzle and ears to the head, head to the body and tail to the body (see page 10 - 12).

HEAD

a) Attach safety eyes after finishing round 23.

1. Place the safety eyes between rounds 16 and 17, leaving 11 stitches (count 10 holes) between.

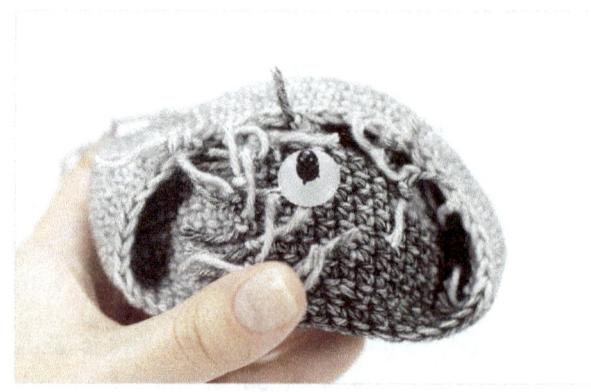

2. Make sure you are satisfied with the placement of the eyes before pushing the washer into place.

b) Embroider the "eyebrows" with white yarn.

Tip! It's much easier to get nice even stitches, if you use a sharp embroidery needle that can go through your stitches rather than having to work around them.

1. Start from the outer side just below round 18. Make a small vertical stitch.

2. Then make the next stitch right next to the first one, but slightly higher.

3. Keep stitching, following the shape of the eye patch.

4. Go all the way up, around the top and back down the other side of the eye patch, finishing just below round 15. Do the same on the other side.

MUZZLE

a) Attach the nose and embroider the mouth.

1. Place the safety nose between rounds 2 and 3.

2. Embroider the mouth before you push the washer into place – this way you can easily get right next to the nose.

EARS

a) Finish the ear pieces, align them and crochet around the edge with single crochet stitches.

1. Align a dark and light gray piece, wrong sides facing. Locate the middle stitch of the first *inc3* and insert the hook from the dark gray side, going through both layers.

2. Attach the white yarn with a slip stitch.

3. Go back into the same stitch, yarn over and draw up a loop.

4. Yarn over...

3. ... and draw through both loops on the hook, completing the first single crochet stitch.

4. Continue crocheting around the two edges with single crochet stitches, going through both layers.

ARMS & LEGS

a) Place the joint or a button inside the arms and legs.

1. Place the disk with a stem inside the limb so the stem is facing straight towards the body.

b) Finish the arms and legs and close the opening.

1. Cut the yarn, leaving a long tail, and fasten off. Thread the yarn tail onto a yarn needle.

2. Insert the needle from the center and under the front loop only and draw the yarn through. Pick up all the remaining stitches onto the yarn.

3. Grab the yarn tail and pull until the hole is tightly closed.

4. Insert the needle through the center, bring the yarn to the side the arm or leg and hide the yarn tail.

ASSEMBLING THE RACCOON

a) Sew the muzzle to the head.

Tip! Sew the ears and muzzle to the head before you sew the head to the body - this way you can fasten all yarn tails securely with a knot under the head.

1. Sew the muzzle to the head with whip stitch, placing it so the top edge is just below round 15.

b) Use yarn to shape the head.

1. Insert the needle from the bottom of the head and bring it up right next to the outer side of the eye.

2. Go about half way around the eye and insert the needle right next to the eye. Bring it to the bottom of the head.

3. Grab the yarn tails and tug gently, pulling the eye in just a bit.

4. Knot the yarn tails together. Do the same with the other eye.

c) Sew the ears to the head.

1. Place the ears just below round 5 of the head.

2. Sew the ears to the head with light gray yarn, inserting the needle through both layers.

d) Finish the arms and legs. Start making the body and attach the limbs as you go.

1. Turn the body so the end of the round is at the center of the back. Attach the legs to either side of the body between rounds 8 and 9.

2. Finish the body. Attach the arms to either side of the body between rounds 23 and 24.

e) Sew the head to the body.

1. Sew the head to the body with whip or mattress stitch (see page 19 - 20). Add a bit more stuffing before closing the seam.

2. Sew the tail to the body with whip or mattress stitch (see page 16 - 18), placing it over rounds 8 - 9.

Small Donkey

CROCHET PATTERN BY KRISTI TULLUS

SIZE

26 cm (10 ¼") including ears, when crocheted with DK weight alpaca and wool blend and a 2,50 mm hook.

SKILLS REQUIRED

Crocheting in spiral, chain, slip and single crochet stitch, increasing and decreasing.

DIFFICULTY

3. Intermediate – includes some less common crochet techniques, color changes and simple shaping.

MATERIALS & TOOLS

- Yarn. I used DROPS 'Lima', a DK weight alpaca-wool blend, 100 m = 50 g (109 yd = 50 g) / 8 ply / 11 wpi / 3: light. You will need about 35 g of gray (#9015), 3 g of white (#0100) and 12 g of black yarn (#8903).
- 2,50 - 3,50 mm crochet hook (US size 2/C - 4/E).
- Polyester fiberfill, wool, wadding etc. for stuffing.
- 8 mm (1/3") safety eyes or buttons, beads, felt etc.
- Two 12 mm (1/2") and two 15 mm (3/5") doll joints or safety eyes or buttons.
- Black cotton embroidery floss.
- Yarn needle, scissors, stitch marker.

CHOOSING JOINTS

Tip! You can use plastic doll joints, safety eyes, cotter pin joints, buttons and thread or even just thread to attach the arms and legs. My favorite are plastic doll joints - they are easy to install, durable and washable. Buttons and thread will work great as well, if you can't get your hands on any joints.

PLASTIC DOLL JOINTS

1. Plastic doll joints come in three pieces - disk with a post, washer and a fastener.

2. Disk with a post is placed inside the limbs, pushing the post through the fabric.

3. And then locked in place inside the body.

BUTTON AND THREAD JOINTS

Tip! Make sure you use very strong thread to attach the limbs – it will have to endure quite a bit of tension and can be a bit difficult to mend, should it break. I have found cotton embroidery floss, nylon sewing thread (doubled or tripled) or fishing line work really well.

1. Cut a length of yarn and draw it through the holes in the button.

2. Place the button inside a limb, drawing the yarn tails through the fabric.

3. Place the other button inside the body, draw the yarn tails through the holes and knot them together.

ABBREVIATIONS

- **st(s)** = stitch(es).
- **mr, sc** *n* = crochet *n* (number) single crochet stitches in to the adjustable loop (see page 12).
- **ch** = chain stitch.
- **sl st** = slip stitch (single crochet stitch in UK and Australia).
- **sc** = single crochet stitch (double crochet stitch in UK and Australia).
- **bpsc** = back post single crochet stitch (see page 11).
- **sc (or sl st, ch etc.)** *n* = crochet *n* single crochet stitches (or sl st, ch etc.), one in each stitch.
- **inc** = increase – crochet two single crochet stitches in the same stitch.
- **dec** = decrease – crochet two stitches together using the invisible decrease method (see page 14).
- **(sc 4, inc) x** *n* = repeat the pattern between parentheses *n* times.
- **(36)** = number of stitches in a round after finishing round.

NOTES

- Work in a continuous spiral, do not join rounds or turn your work, unless instructed otherwise in the pattern.
- Use a stitch marker or a piece of yarn to mark the end or the beginning of a round. Move the marker up after completing each round.
- Work all stitches in both loops, unless instructed otherwise in the pattern.

COPYRIGHT INFO

Copyright © 2019 Kristi Tullus, TÜ Spire. All rights reserved. Contents of this document may not be copied, reproduced, altered, published or distributed in any way. Feel free to sell finished products made with this pattern, I would appreciate a credit as the designer (Kristi Tullus, kristitullus.com).

HEAD

With white yarn:

1: mr, sc 6	(6)
2: inc x 6	(12)
3: (inc, sc) x 6	(18)
4: (sc 5, inc) x 3	(21)
5: sc in each st	(21)
6: sc 2, inc, (sc 6, inc) x 2, sc 4	(24)
7: sc in each st	(24)

With gray yarn:

8: (sc 7, inc) x 3	(27)

On round 9 place a stitch marker between stitches 14 and 15 (around the loops of the 15th stitch) to mark the center of the face. Use it as guide when placing the eyes.

9: sc 3, inc, (sc 8, inc) x 2, sc 5	(30)
10: (sc 4, inc) x 6	(36)
11: sc 12, inc, (sc 2, inc) x 3, sc 14	(40)
12: sc 15, inc, sc 7, inc, sc 16	(42)

Attach safety eyes between rounds 9 and 10, leaving 10 stitches (count 9 holes) between them (see page 6).

13-19: sc in each st	(42)
20: sc 12, dec, sc 19, dec, sc 7	(40)
21: (sc 8, dec) x 4	(36)
22: sc, dec, (sc 4, dec) x 5, sc 3	(30)

Start stuffing the head. Keep adding a bit of fiberfill after every few rounds, stuffing the head firmly.

23: (sc 3, dec) x 6	(24)
24: (dec, sc 2) x 6	(18)
25: (sc, dec) x 6	(12)
26: dec x 6	(6)

Finish stuffing the head. Cut the yarn, leaving a long yarn tail, and fasten off. Pick up all the remaining stitches and close the opening (see page 6).

EARS (make 2)

With gray yarn:

1: mr, sc 6	(6)

...

2: (inc, sc) x 3	(9)
3: (sc 2, inc) x 3	(12)
4: sc, inc, (sc 3, inc) x 2, sc 2	(15)
5: (sc 4, inc) x 3	(18)
6: sc 2, inc, (sc 5, inc) x 2, sc 3	(21)
7-11: sc in each st	(21)
12: sc 4, dec, sc 15	(20)
13: sc in each st	(20)

Sl st in next stitch. Cut the yarn, leaving a long yarn tail for sewing, and fasten off. Do not stuff the ears.

ARMS (make 2)

With black yarn:

1: mr, sc 6	(6)
2: inc x 6	(12)
3: (sc, inc) x 6	(18)
4: bpsc in each st	(18)
5: sc 6, dec, sc 2, dec, sc 6	(16)
6: sc 7, dec, sc 7	(15)
7: sc 3, dec, sc 6, dec, sc 2	(13)

Stuff firmly. Keep adding a bit of fiberfill after every few rounds, stuffing the arms firmly.

With gray yarn:

8: sc 6, dec, sc 5	(12)
9: sc in each st	(12)
10: sc 6, dec, sc 4	(11)
11: sc in each st	(11)
12: sc 6, dec, sc 3	(10)
13-20: sc in each st	(10)

On the right arm only, sc in next five stitches. Count the last sc as the end of the round from now on.

21: sc 8, dec	(9)

Attach the smaller joint between rounds 20 and 21, placing it so the stem is facing straight towards the body (see page 8).

22: (dec, sc) x 3	(6)

Finish stuffing. Cut the yarn, leaving a long yarn tail, and fasten off. Pick up all the remaining stitches and close the opening (see page 6).

LEGS (make 2)

With black yarn:

1: mr, sc 6	(6)
2: inc x 6	(12)
3: (sc, inc) x 6	(18)
4: (inc, sc 2) x 6	(24)
5: bpsc in each st	(24)
6: sc 5, dec, (sc 4, dec) x 2, sc 5	(21)
7: sc 7, dec, sc 4, dec, sc 6	(19)
8: dec, sc 7, dec, sc 8	(17)
9: sc 4, dec, sc 6, dec, sc 3	(15)

Stuff firmly. Keep adding a bit of fiberfill after every few rounds, stuffing the legs firmly.

With gray yarn:

10: sc 5, dec, sc 2, dec, sc 4	(13)
11: sc in each st	(13)
12: sc 6, dec, sc 5	(12)
13: sc in each st	(12)
14: sc 6, dec, sc 4	(11)
15-24: sc in each st	(11)

On the right leg only, sc in next 5 stitches. Count the last sc as the end of the round from now on.

Attach the larger joint between rounds 21 and 22, placing it so the stem is facing straight towards the body (see page 8).

25: sc, dec x 5	(6)

Finish stuffing. Cut the yarn, leaving a long yarn tail, and fasten off. Pick up all the remaining stitches and close the opening (see page 6).

BODY

With gray yarn:

1: mr, sc 6	(6)
2: inc x 6	(12)
3: (sc, inc) x 6	(18)
4: (inc, sc 2) x 6	(24)
5: (sc 3, inc) x 6	(30)
6: sc 6, inc, (sc 9, inc) x 2, sc 3	(33)
7-11: sc in each st	(33)

...

Turn the body so the end of the round is at the center of your donkey's back. Attach the legs to the sides of the body, between rounds 7 and 8 (see page 9).

12: sc 4, dec, (sc 9, dec) x 2, sc 5	(30)
13: (sc 8, dec) x 3	(27)
14: sc in each st	(27)
15: sc 10. dec, sc 4, dec, sc 9	(25)

Start stuffing the body. Keep adding a bit of fiberfill after every few rounds, stuffing the body firmly

16: sc 6, dec, sc 11, dec, sc 4	(23)
17: sc 11, dec, sc 10	(22)
18: dec, sc 20	(21)
19: sc 5, dec, sc 8, dec, sc 4	(19)
20: sc 7, dec, sc 3, dec, sc 5	(17)
21: dec, sc 15	(16)
22-23: sc in each st	(16)
24: sc 4, leave the rest of the sts unworked	(16)

Sl st in next stitch. Cut the yarn, leaving a long yarn tail for sewing, and fasten off.

Attach the arms to the the sides of the body, between rounds 19 and 20 (see page 9).

Finish stuffing the body.

TAIL

With gray yarn:

1: mr, sc 5	(5)
2-3: sc in each st	(5)

Start stuffing the tail. Keep adding a bit of fiberfill after every few rounds, stuffing the tail lightly.

4: sc 2, inc, sc 2	(6)
5-7: sc in each st	(6)

Sl st in next stitch. Cut the yarn, leaving a long yarn tail for sewing, and fasten off. Finish stuffing the tail.

HEAD

a) Attach safety eyes after finishing round 12.

1. Place the eyes to either side of the stitch marker, between rounds 9 and 10, leaving 10 stitches (count 9 holes) between them.

2. Make sure you are satisfied with the placement of the eyes before pushing the washer into place.

b) Finish the head and close the opening.

1. Cut the yarn, leaving a long tail, and fasten off. Thread the yarn tail onto a yarn needle.

2. Pick up all the remaining stitches onto the yarn, inserting the needle from the center and under the front loop only and draw the yarn through.

3. Grab the yarn tail and pull until the hole is tightly closed.

4. Insert the needle through the center and bring the yarn to the bottom of the head. Fasten and hide the yarn tail.

c) Use yarn to shape the head.

1. Insert the needle from the bottom of the head, between rounds 13 and 15, and bring it up right next to the outer side of the eye.

2. Go about half way around the eye and insert the needle right next to the inner side of the eye. Bring it to the bottom of the head.

3. Grab the yarn tails and tug gently, pulling the eye in just a bit.

4. Knot the yarn tails together. Do the same with the other eye.

d) Embroider the nostrils.

1. Embroider the nostrils, making a few stitches over round 4 with black embroidery floss.

2. Leave about 4 - 5 stitches between the two nostrils.

ARMS & LEGS

a) Place the joint or a button inside the arms and legs.

1. Place the disk inside the limb so the stem is facing straight towards the body.

2. Finish the arms and legs and close the opening (see page 6).

ASSEMBLING THE DONKEY

a) Sew the ears to the head.

1. Flatten the ears and fold them in half lengthwise.

2. Place the ears just behind round 14 of the head, leaving 9 - 10 stitches between them.

3. Start sewing the ear to the head.

4. When you reach the center, fold the ear in half and sew the second side next to the first.

b) Finish the arms and legs. Start making the body and attach the limbs as you go.

1. Turn the body so the end of the round is at the center of the back. Attach the legs to either side of the body between rounds 7 and 8.

2. Finish the body. Attach the arms to the sides of the body between rounds 19 and 20.

c) Sew the head to the body.

1. Sew the head to the body with whip stitch (see page 15), placing it so the front edge is just behind round 11 of the head.

2. Add a bit more stuffing before closing the seam.

d) Sew the tail to the body.

1. Sew the tail to the body with whip or mattress stitch (see page 15 - 17), placing it just above round 6 of the body.

MANE & TAIL

a) Make the mane and finish the tail.

1. Cut about 6 cm long pieces of yarn for the mane and 9 cm long pieces for the tail.

2. Insert the hook under a stitch. Fold a piece of yarn in half, grab the center and draw up a loop.

3. Use your hook to draw both yarn tails through the loop.

4. Grab the yarn tails and pull gently, drawing the loop tight.

5. Start attaching the mane at round 13, go around the head and four rows down the back. Make it about three stitches wide, following the color of the stripes.

6. Attach longer yarn pieces over the first two rounds of the tail using the same method.

Christmas Teddy Bear

Crochet pattern by Kristi Tullus

Size
20.5 cm (8"), with DK weight cotton-linen blend and a 2,50 mm crochet hook (US size 2/B).

Skills required
Crocheting in spiral, chain, slip, single and double crochet stitch, increasing and decreasing.

Difficulty
3. Intermediate – includes some less common crochet techniques and color changes.

Contact Info
Pattern includes unlimited support from me over email or Skype. Crochet photo and video tutorials and helpful tips are available on my website.

 kristi@spire.ee    http://sidrun.spire.ee    a0kristi

Copyright © 2016 TÜ Spire. Contents of this document MAY NOT be copied, reproduced, altered, published or distributed in any way. You MAY sell finished products made with this pattern, provided you credit me as the designer (KristiTullus, http://spire.ee/).

Tip! You can use the same pattern to make larger or smaller toys by using finer or bulkier yarn. Make sure to pick a crochet hook at least a size smaller than suggested on the yarn label and crochet tightly enough to achieve a tight gauge that will not allow the stuffing to show through the fabric. You may also need to adjust the size of the safety eyes, nose and joints.

Materials & Tools

- Yarn. I used DK weight cotton and linen blend, 112 m = 50 g (122 yd = 50 g) / 8 ply / 11 wpi / 3: light. You will need about 55 g of beige, 60 g of red and 6 g of white yarn.
- 2,50 - 3,00 mm crochet hook (US size 1/B - 3/D) or according to the yarn.
- Polyester fiberfill, wool, wadding for stuffing.
- 9 mm (1/3") safety eyes or buttons, beads, felt etc.
- Two 20 mm (4/5") and two 15 mm (3/5") plastic doll joints or safety eyes or buttons and thread.
- Embroidery floss.
- Yarn needle, scissors, stitch marker.

Choosing joints

Tip! You can use plastic doll joints, cotter pin joints, buttons and thread or even just thread to attach the arms and legs. My favorite are plastic doll joints - they are easy to install, durable and waterproof. Buttons and thread will work great as well, if you can't get your hands on any joints.

Plastic doll joints

1. Plastic doll joints come in three pieces - disk with a stem, washer and a fastener. You can also use safety eyes.

2. Disk with a stem is placed inside the limbs, pushing the stem through the fabric.

3. And then locked to place inside the body.

53

Christmas Teddy Bear | EN-076 | Copyright © 2016 TU Spire | http://spire.ee

Button and thread joints

Tip! Make sure you use a very strong thread to attach the limbs – it will have to endure quite a bit of tension and can be a bit difficult to mend, should it break. I have found cotton embroidery floss, nylon sewing thread (doubled or tripled) or fishing line work really well.

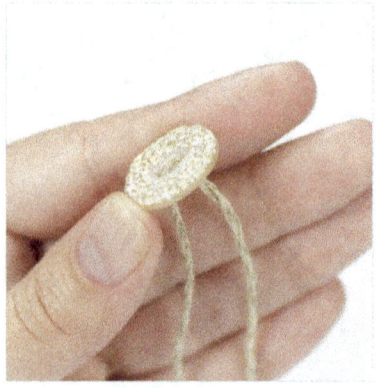

1. Cut a length of yarn and draw it through the holes in the button.

2. Place the button inside a limb, drawing the yarn tails through the fabric.

3. Place the other button inside the body, draw the yarn tails through the holes and knot them together.

Abbreviations

- **st(s)** = stitch(es).
- **mr, sc** *n* = crochet *n* (number) single crochet stitches in to the adjustable loop (see page 13).
- **ch** = chain stitch.
- **sl st** = slip stitch (single crochet stitch in UK and Australia).
- **sc** = single crochet stitch (double crochet stitch in UK and Australia).
- **dc** = double crochet stitch (triple crochet stitch in UK and Australia).
- **sc (or sl st, ch, hdc etc.)** *n* = make *n* single crochet stitches (or sl st, ch, hdc etc.), one in each stitch.
- **inc** = increase – crochet two single crochet stitches in the same stitch.
- **inc3** = double increase – crochet three single crochet stitches in the same stitch.
- **dec** = decrease – crochet two stitches together using the invisible decrease method (see page 15).
- **(sc 4, inc) x** *n* = repeat the pattern between parentheses *n* times.
- **(36)** = number of stitches in a round after finishing round.

Notes

- Work in a continuous spiral, do not join rounds or turn your work, unless instructed otherwise in the pattern.
- All stitches are worked into both loops, unless instructed otherwise in the pattern.
- Make sure to crochet tightly enough to achieve a tight gauge that will not allow the stuffing to show through the fabric.
- Use a stitch marker or a piece of yarn to mark the end or the beginning of a round. Move the marker up after completing each round.

Head

With beige yarn:

1: mr, sc 6	(6)
2: inc x 6	(12)
3: (sc, inc) x 6	(18)
4: (inc, sc 2) x 6	(24)
5: (sc 3, inc) x 6	(30)
6: sc, inc, (sc 4, inc) x 5, sc 3	(36)
7: (sc 5, inc) x 6	(42)
8: sc 2, inc, (sc 6, inc) x 5, sc 4	(48)
9: (sc 7, inc) x 6	(54)
10-18: sc in each st	(54)
19: (sc 7, dec) x 6	(48)
20: sc 2, dec, (sc 6, dec) x 5, sc 4	(42)

Attach safety eyes between rows 15 and 16, leaving 10 stitches (count 9 holes) between them (see page 7).

Start stuffing the head. Keep adding a bit of fiberfill after every few rounds, stuffing the head firmly.

21: (sc 5, dec) x 6	(36)
22: sc, dec, (sc 4, dec) x 5, sc 3	(30)
23: (sc 3, dec) x 6	(24)
24: (dec, sc 2) x 6	(18)

Sl st in next stitch. Cut the yarn, leaving a long yarn tail for sewing, and fasten off. Stuff the head firmly.

Muzzle

With white yarn:

1: mr, sc 6	(6)
2: (inc3 x 2, sc) x 2	(14)
3: sc 2, inc x 3, sc 4, inc x 3, sc 2	(20)
4-5: sc in each st	(20)

Sl st in next stitch. Cut the yarn, leaving a long yarn tail for sewing, and fasten off. Stuff the muzzle firmly.

Ear

With beige yarn:

1: mr, sc 6	(6)
2: inc x 6	(12)
3: (sc 2, inc) x 4	(16)

...

4-6: sc in each st	(16)

Sl st in next stitch. Cut the yarn, leaving a long yarn tail for sewing, and fasten off.

Hat

With red yarn:

1: mr, sc 6	(6)
2: sc in each st	(6)
3: (sc 2, inc) x 2	(8)
4: sc in each st	(8)
5: sc, inc, sc 3, inc, sc 2	(10)
6: sc in each st	(10)
7: (sc 4, inc) x 2	(12)
8: sc in each st	(12)
9: sc 2, inc, sc 5, inc, sc 3	(14)
10: sc in each st	(14)
11: (sc 6, inc) x 2	(16)
12: sc in each st	(16)
13: sc 3, inc, sc 7, inc, sc 4	(18)
14: sc in each st	(18)
15: (sc 8, inc) x 2	(20)
16: sc in each st	(20)
17: sc 4, inc, sc 9, inc, sc 5	(22)
18: sc in each st	(22)
19: (sc 10, inc) x 2	(24)
20: sc in each st	(24)
21: sc 5, inc, sc 11, inc, sc 6	(26)
22: sc in each st	(26)
23: (sc 12, inc) x 2	(28)
24: sc in each st	(28)
25: sc 6, inc, sc 13, inc, sc 7	(30)
26-32: sc in each st	(30)
33: (sc 4, inc) x 6	(36)
34: sc in each st	(36)
35: sc 2, inc, (sc 5, inc) x 5, sc 3	(42)
36: sc in each st	(42)
37: (sc 6, inc) x 6	(48)
38: sc in each st	(48)
39: sc 3, inc, (sc 7, inc) x 5, sc 4	(54)
40: sc in each st	(54)
41: (sc 8, inc) x 6	(60)
42-43: sc in each st	(60)

Sl st in next stitch. Cut the yarn, leaving a long yarn tail for sewing, and fasten off.

Legs (make 2)

With beige yarn:

1: ch 7, 2 sc in second ch from hook, sc 4, 4 sc in first ch

Rotate and work on other side of beginning chain.

   sc 4, 2 sc in last ch   (16)

Keep working in spiral.

2: inc, sc 5, inc3, sc 2, inc3, sc 5, inc   (22)
3: inc3, sc 7, inc3, sc 4, inc3, sc 8   (28)

Work in back loops only on round 4!

4-5: sc in each st   (28)
6: sc, dec, sc 25   (27)
7: sc 8, dec x 3, sc, dec x 3, sc 6   (21)
8: sc 7, dec x 2, sc, dec x 2, sc 5   (17)
9: sc 6, dec x 3, sc 5   (14)
10: sc 7, dec, sc 5   (13)

Stuff the feet firmly. Keep adding a bit of fiberfill after every few rounds, stuffing the legs firmly.

11-17: sc in each st   (13)

On the left leg only, crochet *sc* in next 6 stitches. Count the last *sc* as the end of the round from now on.

Attach the disk with a stem between rows 16 and 17, placing it so the stem is facing straight towards the body (see page 8).

18: dec, sc 6, dec, sc 3   (11)
19: sc, dec x 5   (6)

Finish stuffing. Cut the yarn, leaving a long yarn tail, and fasten off. Close the opening (see page 8 - 9).

Right arm

With beige yarn:

1: mr, sc 6   (6)
2: (inc3 x 2, sc) x 2   (14)
3: sc 3, inc, sc 6, inc, sc 3   (16)
4-5: sc in each st   (16)
6: sc 2, dec x 2, sc 6, inc, sc 3   (15)
...

7: sc 2, dec, sc 6, inc, sc 4   (15)
8: sc, dec x 2, sc 10   (13)
9: sc, dec, sc 10   (12)

Stuff the hands firmly. Keep adding a bit of fiberfill after every few rounds, stuffing the arms firmly.

With red yarn:

10-13: sc in each st   (12)
14: sc, dec, sc 9   (11)
15-20: sc in each st   (11)

Attach the disk with a stem between rows 19 and 20, placing it so the stem is facing straight towards the body (see page 8).

21: sc 9, dec   (10)
22: dec x 5   (5)

Finish stuffing. Cut the yarn, leaving a long yarn tail, and fasten off. Close the opening (see page 8 - 9).

Crochet a row of slip stitches between rounds 9 and 10 (see page 9 - 10).

Left arm

With beige yarn:

1: mr, sc 6   (6)
2: (inc3 x 2, sc) x 2   (14)
3: sc 3, inc, sc 6, inc, sc 3   (16)
4-5: sc in each st   (16)
6: sc 4, inc, sc 6, dec x 2, sc   (15)
7: sc 5, inc, sc 6, dec, sc   (15)

Crochet one *sc* in next two stitches and count the last *sc* as the end of the round from now on.

8: sc 10, dec x 2, sc   (13)
9: sc 10, dec, sc   (12)

Stuff the hands firmly. Keep adding a bit of fiberfill after every few rounds, stuffing the arms firmly.

With red yarn:

10-13: sc in each st   (12)
...

...

14: sc 10, dec	(11)
15-21: sc in each st	(11)

Attach the disk with a stem between rows 20 and 21, placing it so the stem is facing straight towards the body (see page 8).

22: sc 3, dec x 4	(7)
23: dec x 2, leave rest of the sts unworked	(5)

Finish stuffing. Cut the yarn, leaving a long yarn tail, and fasten off. Close the opening (see page 8 - 9).

Crochet a row of slip stitches between rounds 9 and 10 (see page 9 - 10).

Body

With beige yarn:

1: mr, sc 6	(6)
2: inc x 6	(12)
3: (sc, inc) x 6	(18)
4: (inc, sc 2) x 6	(24)
5: (sc 3, inc) x 6	(30)
6: sc, inc, (sc 4, inc) x 5, sc 3	(36)
7: (sc 5, inc) x 6	(42)
8-13: sc in each st	(42)

Turn the body so the last stitch of round 13 is facing away from you (center of the back). Attach the legs to either side of the body, between rows 8 and 9 (see page 9).

14: sc 11, switch to red yarn, sc 31	(42)
15: sc 9, dec, sc 5, dec, sc 6, dec, sc 5, dec, sc 9	(38)
16: sc 18, dec, sc 16, dec	(36)
17: (sc 11, dec) x 2, sc 10	(34)
18: sc 3, dec, sc 25, dec, sc 2	(32)

Start stuffing the body. Keep adding a bit of fiberfill after every few rounds, stuffing the body firmly.

19: sc 16, dec, sc 14	(31)
20: dec, sc 29	(30)
21: sc 7, dec, sc 13, dec, sc 6	(28)

...

22: sc 10, dec, sc 6, dec, sc 8	(26)
23: (dec, sc 11) x 2	(24)
24: sc 6, dec, sc 10, dec, sc 4	(22)
25: sc 9, dec, sc 2, dec, sc 7	(20)
26: dec, sc 8, dec, sc 5, switch to beige yarn, sc 3	(18)
27-28: sc in each st	(18)

Sl st in next stitch. Cut the yarn and fasten off. Attach the arms to either side of the body between rows 23 and 24. Finish stuffing the body.

Crochet a row of slip stitches between rounds 13 and 14 (see page 9 - 10).

Scarf

Tip! The edge will look nicer if you crochet all *dc*-s into the loops on the back of the starting chain (see page 12).

With white yarn:

1: ch 53, starting in 4th ch from hook, dc 49, ch 3, sl st in 1st ch

Fasten off and weave in the yarn tails.

Head

a) Attach safety eyes after finishing round 20.

1. Place the eyes between rows 15 and 16 leaving 10 stitches (count 9 holes) between them.

2. Make sure you are satisfied with the placement of the eyes before pushing the washer into place.

b) Sew the muzzle to the head.

Tip! It is difficult to stuff a large open piece. I find it easiest to start pinning the muzzle to the head and add stuffing as you go.

1. Start pinning the muzzle to the head, start adding fiberfill when you are about half way around it.

2. Sew the muzzle to the head (see page 17).

c) Embroider the nose.

1. Insert the needle from the bottom of the head, leaving a short yarn tail. Make a long vertical stitch.

2. Bring the yarn up where you want the nose to start and make horizontal stitches to form the nose.

Christmas Teddy Bear | EN-076 | Copyright © 2016 TU Spire | http://spire.ee

3. Keep stitching until the nose is big enough.

4. Come back out through the opening under the head and knot the yarn ends together.

Arms & Legs

a) Place the disk with a stem or a button inside the arms and legs.

1. Place the disk inside the limb so the stem is facing straight towards the body.

2. Or use a button instead, placing it the same way.

b) Finish the arms and legs and close the opening.

1. Cut the yarn, leaving a long tail, and fasten off. Thread the yarn tail onto a yarn needle.

2. Pick up all the remaining stitches onto the yarn, inserting the needle from the center and under the front loop only and draw the yarn through.

3. Grab the yarn tail and pull until the hole is tightly closed.

4. Insert the needle through the center and bring the yarn to the side of the limb. Hide the yarn tail.

Body

a) Finish the arms and legs. Start making the body and attach the limbs as you go.

1. Turn the body so the end of the round is at the center of the back. Attach the legs to either side of the body between rounds 8 and 9.

2. Finish the body. Attach the arms to either side of the body between rounds 23 and 24.

b) Finish the body. Crochet a row of slip stitches between rounds 15 and 16.

1. Turn the body upside down. Insert your hook under the first stitch. Grab the yarn and draw up a loop.

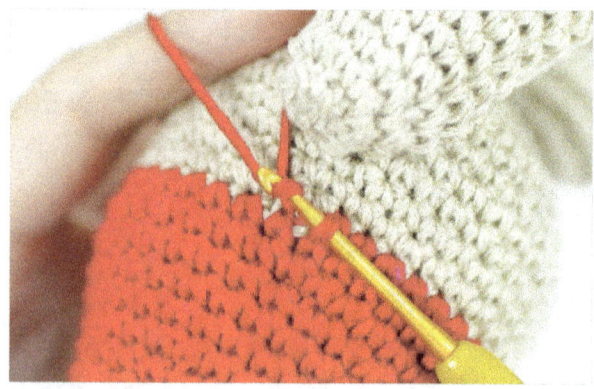
2. Yarn over..

3. ... and draw through the loop on the hook.

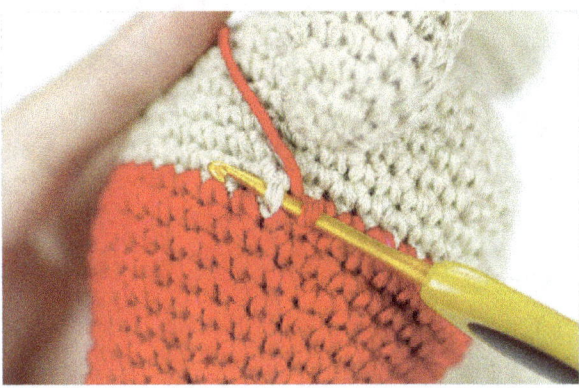

4. Insert the hook under the next stitch and yarn over.

5. Draw the yarn under the stitch and through the loop on the hook.

6. Continue around the body, repeating steps 4 and 5.

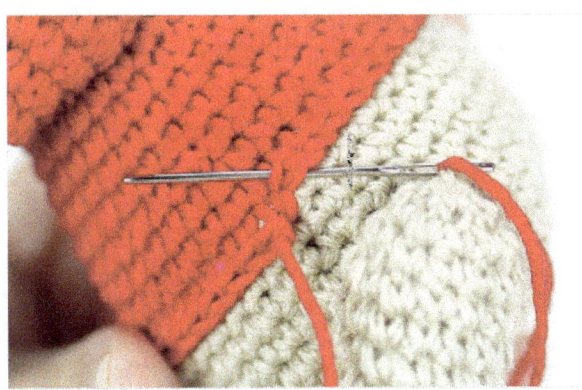

7. Cut the yarn and fasten off. Thread the yarn tail onto a needle. Insert the needle under both loops of the first stitch and draw the yarn through.

8. Insert the needle between the two loops of the last stitch and bring it up through the opening.

9. Tug the yarn tail gently until the loop is about the same size as other stitches. Knot the yarn ends together.

10. Do the same with the arms.

Assembling the bear

a) Sew the ear and hat to the head.

Tip! Sew the muzzle, ear and hat to the head and embroider the nose before you sew the head to the body - this way you can fasten all yarn tails securely with a knot under the head.

1. Place the ear just below round 6 of the head.

2. Push the ear flat and sew it to the head, inserting the needle through both layers.

3. Pin the hat to the head, turning it so the end of the round is on your bear's left side. Sew the hat to the head with back stitch just above the last round.

4. Fold the tip of the hat down, covering the place where the last round ends, and sew it to the head, making a few stitches through the hat.

c) Sew the head to the body.

1. Sew the head to the body (see page 17).

2. Add a bit more stuffing before closing the seam.

Scarf

Tip! The edge of the scarf will look nicer if you crochet all double crochet stitches into the loops on the back of the starting chain.

1. Front of the chain, showing the V-shaped stitches.

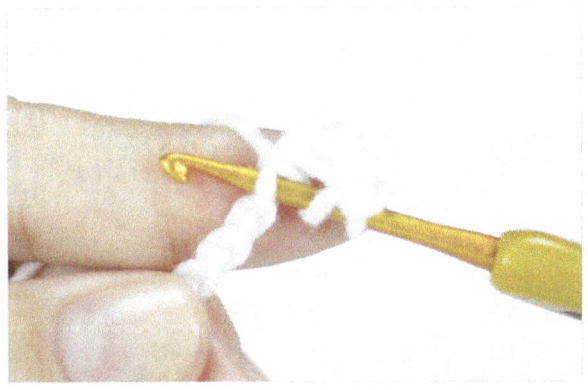

2. Flip the chain over and insert the hook through the loops on the back of the chain.

3. This will leave a nice row of loops along the edge.

4. Finish the scarf and weave in the yarn tails. Tie the hat around your bear's neck.

Christmas Teddy Bear | EN-076 | Copyright © 2016 TÜ Spire | http://spire.ee

Long-Legged Bunny

Kristi Tullus

Size
27 cm (10 2/3"), when crocheted with DK weight cotton-acrylic blend and a 2,50 mm hook.

Skills required
Crocheting in spiral, chain, slip and single crochet stitch, increasing and decreasing.

Difficulty
2. Beginner – works up using only single crochet stitches, includes some less common crochet techniques.

Contact Info
Pattern includes unlimited support from me over email (kristi@spire.ee). Photo and video tutorials and tips are available on my website https://kristitullus.com

Copyright © 2012 TÜ Spire. Contents of this document MAY NOT be copied, reproduced, altered, published or distributed in any way. You MAY sell finished products made with this pattern, I would appreciate a credit as the designer (Kristi Tullus, kristitullus.com).

Tip! You can use the same pattern to make larger or smaller toys by using finer or bulkier yarn. Make sure to pick a crochet hook at least a size smaller than suggested on the yarn label and crochet tightly enough to achieve a tight gauge that will not allow the stuffing to show through the fabric. You may also need to adjust the size of the safety eyes, nose and joints.

Materials & Tools

- Yarn. I used Scheepjes 'Stone Washed', a sport weight cotton and acrylic blend, 130 m = 50 g (142 yd = 50 g) / 12 wpi / 2: fine. You will need about 68 g of yarn.
- 2,50 - 3,50 mm crochet hook (US size 2/C - 4/E) or according to the yarn.
- Polyester fiberfill, wool, wadding for stuffing.
- 9 mm (1/3") safety eyes or buttons, beads, felt etc.
- Yarn needle, scissors, stitch marker.

Abbreviations

- **st(s)** = stitch(es).
- **mr, sc *n*** = magic ring - start with an adjustable loop and crochet *n* (number) single crochet stitches into the adjustable loop (see page 8).
- **ch** = chain stitch.
- **sl st** = slip stitch (single crochet stitch in UK and Australia).
- **sc** = single crochet stitch (double crochet stitch in UK and Australia).
- **sc (or sl st, ch, hdc etc.) *n*** = make *n* single crochet stitches (or sl st, ch, hdc etc.), one in each stitch.
- **inc** = increase – crochet two single crochet stitches in the same stitch.
- **inc3** = double increase – crochet three single crochet stitches in the same stitch.
- **dec** = decrease – crochet two stitches together using the invisible decrease method (see page 10).
- **(sc 4, inc) x *n*** = repeat the pattern between parentheses *n* times.
- **(36)** = number of stitches in a round after finishing round.

Notes

- Work in a continuous spiral, do not join rounds or turn your work, unless instructed otherwise in the pattern.
- Use a stitch marker or a piece of yarn to mark the end or the beginning of a round. Move the marker up after completing each round.
- Work all stitches in both loops, unless instructed otherwise in the pattern.

Head

1: mr, sc 6	(6)
2: inc x 6	(12)
3: (sc, inc) x 6	(18)
4: (inc, sc 2) x 6	(24)
5: (sc 3, inc) x 6	(30)
6: sc, inc, (sc 4, inc) x 5, sc 3	(36)
7: (sc 5, inc) x 6	(42)
8: sc 2, inc, (sc 6, inc) x 5, sc 4	(48)
9: (sc 7, inc) x 6	(54)
10-19: sc in each stitch	(54)
20: (sc 7, dec) x 6	(48)
21: sc 2, dec, (sc 6, dec) x 5, sc 4	(42)

Attach safety eyes between rows 17 and 18, leaving 11 stitches (count 10 holes) between them.

Start stuffing the head. Keep adding a bit of fiberfill after every few rounds, stuffing the head firmly.

22: (sc 5, dec) x 6	(36)
23: sc, dec, (sc 4, dec) x 5, sc 3	(30)
24: (sc 3, dec) x 6	(24)
25: (dec, sc) x 8	(16)

Sl st in next stitch. Cut the yarn, leaving a long yarn tail for sewing, and fasten off. Stuff the head firmly.

Body

1: mr, sc 6	(6)
2: inc x 6	(12)
3: (sc, inc) x 6	(18)
4: (inc, sc 2) x 6	(24)
5: (sc 3, inc) x 6	(30)
6: sc, inc, (sc 4, inc) x 5, sc 3	(36)
7-11: sc in each stitch	(36)
12: (sc 10, dec) x 3	(33)
13: sc in each st	(33)
14: sc 4, dec, (sc 9, dec) x 2, sc 5	(30)

Start stuffing the body. Keep adding a bit of fiberfill after every few rounds, stuffing the body firmly.

15: sc in each st	(30)
16: (sc 8, dec) x 3	(27)
17: sc in each st	(27)

...

18: sc 3, dec, (sc 7, dec) x 2, sc 4	(24)
19: sc in each st	(24)
20: (sc 6, dec) x 3	(21)
21: sc in each st	(21)
22: (sc 2, dec) x 5, sc	(16)
23: sc in each st	(16)

Sl st in next stitch. Cut the yarn, fasten off and hide the yarn tail. Stuff the body firmly.

Arms (make 2)

1: mr, sc 6	(6)
2: inc x 6	(12)
3: (sc 2, inc) x 4	(16)
4-6: sc in each st	(16)
7: (dec, sc 2) x 4	(12)
8: (sc 4, dec) x 2	(10)

Stuff the hands firmly. Keep adding a bit of fiberfill after every few rounds, stuffing the arms lightly about half way up.

9: sc in each st	(10)
10: sc 4, dec, sc 4	(9)
11-12: sc in each st	(9)
13: sc 4, dec, sc 3	(8)
14-21: sc in each st	(8)
22: sc 5, flatten and sc through both layers (see page 5 - 6).	

Cut the yarn, leaving a long yarn tail for sewing, and fasten off.

Legs (make 2)

1: ch 7, 2 sc in 2nd ch from hook, sc 4, 4 sc in first ch

Rotate and work on other side of beginning chain.

sc 4, 2 sc in last ch	(16)

Continue crocheting in spiral.

2: inc, sc 5, inc3, sc 2, inc3, sc 5, inc	(22)
3: inc3, sc 7, inc3, sc 4, inc3, sc 8	(28)

...

...

Work in back loops only on round 4!

4-5: sc in each st	(28)
6: sc, dec, sc 25	(27)
7: sc 9, dec x 6, sc 6	(21)
8: sc 4, dec, sc 3, dec x 3, sc 3, dec, sc	(16)
9: sc 7, dec, sc, dec, sc 4	(13)
10: sc 6, dec x 2, sc 4	(12)

Stuff the feet firmly. Keep adding a bit of fiberfill after every few rounds, stuffing the legs lightly.

11: sc in each st	(12)
12: sc 7, dec, sc 3	(11)
13: sc in each st	(11)
14: sc 7, dec, sc 2	(10)
15-29: sc in each st	(10)
30: (sc, dec) x 3, sc	(7)

Sl st in next stitch. Cut the yarn, leaving a long yarn tail for sewing, and fasten off. Finish stuffing the legs.

Ears (make 2)

1: mr, sc 6	(6)
2: inc x 6	(12)
3: (sc, inc) x 6	(18)
4: (inc, sc 2) x 6	(24)
5: (sc 3, inc) x 6	(30)
6: sc, inc, (sc 4, inc) x 5, sc 3	(36)
7-8: sc in each st	(36)
9: (dec, sc 16) x 2	(34)
10: sc in each st	(34)
11: (dec, sc 15) x 2	(32)
12: sc in each st	(32)
13: (dec, sc 14) x 2	(30)
14: sc in each st	(30)
15: (dec, sc 13) x 2	(28)
16: sc in each st	(28)
17: (dec, sc 12) x 2	(26)
18: sc in each st	(26)
19: (dec, sc 11) x 2	(24)
20: sc in each st	(24)
21: (dec, sc 10) x 2	(22)

...

22: sc in each st	(22)
23: (dec, sc 9) x 2	(20)
24: sc in each st	(20)
25: (dec, sc 8) x 2	(18)
26: sc in each st	(18)
27: sc, flatten and sc through both layers (see page 5 - 6).	

Cut the yarn, leaving a long yarn tail for sewing, and fasten off.

Tail

1: mr, sc 6	(6)
2: inc x 6	(12)
3: (inc, sc 2) x 4	(16)
4: (sc 3, inc) x 4	(20)
5-6: sc in each st	(20)
7: (sc, dec x 2) x 4	(12)

Sl st in next stitch. Cut the yarn, leaving a long yarn tail for sewing, and fasten off. Stuff the tail firmly.

Head

a) Attach safety eyes after finishing round 21.

1. Place the eyes between rows 17 and 18, leaving 11 stitches (count 10 holes) between them.

2. Make sure you are satisfied with the placement of the eyes before pushing the washer into place.

b) Embroider the nose.

1. Insert the needle from the bottom of the head and bring it up between the eyes. Start by making a long vertical stitch.

2. Make small horizontal stitches to form the nose. Keep stitching until the nose is big enough. Come back out to the bottom and knot the yarn ends together.

Arms & Ears

a) Close the opening by crocheting over it with single crochet stitches.

1. Push the top flat and insert the crochet hook through both layers.

2. Yarn over and draw up a loop. Yarn over ...

3. ... and draw through both loops on the hook, completing a single crochet stitch.

4. Crochet over the whole opening. Cut the yarn, leaving a long tail for sewing, and fasten off.

Assembling the Bunny

a) Sew the head, arms, legs and tail to the body and ears to the head.

Tip! Use sewing pins to attach the details to the head and body before sewing to find the right place and get a symmetrical result.

1. Sew the head to the body with mattress stitch (see page 9).

2. Add a bit more stuffing before closing the seam.

3. Sew the arms to the sides of the body, one row below the head.

4. Sew the legs to the body over round 6, leaving 8 - 9 stitches (count 7 - 8 holes) between them.

5. Sew the tail to the body over rounds 6-9.

6. Sew the ears to the sides of the head, just below round 12.

Crochet Stitches

BACK POST SINGLE CROCHET STITCH

Instead of crocheting single crochet stitches around the loops on top of a stitch, crochet them around the post (vertical bar), inserting the hook from the back and going over the stitch.

1. Insert the hook through the stitch from back to front, on the right of the post, going under both loops.

2. Go over the post of the stitch and bring the hook to the back of your work on the other side of the post.

3. So now you have the post of the stitch on the hook.

4. Yarn over...

5. ... and draw up a loop. Yarn over...

6. ... and draw through both loops on the hook, completing the single crochet stitch.

Amigurumi Essentials

MAGIC RING

A magic ring is a way to begin crocheting in round by crocheting the first round into an adjustable loop and then pulling the loop tight. Alternatively you can chain 2 and then crochet the first round into the second chain from hook.

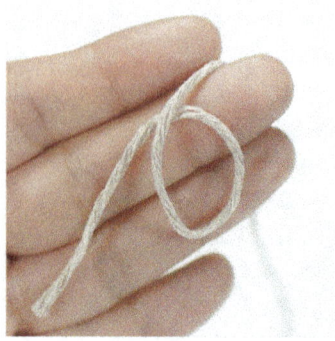

1. Make a loop about 2 cm / 1" from the yarn end so the working yarn goes over the yarn tail.

2. Grab the join between your thumb and forefinger and insert the hook through the loop from front to back.

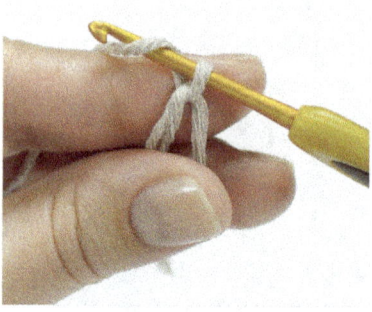

3. Yarn over and pull up a loop. Yarn over and pull through the loop on the hook.

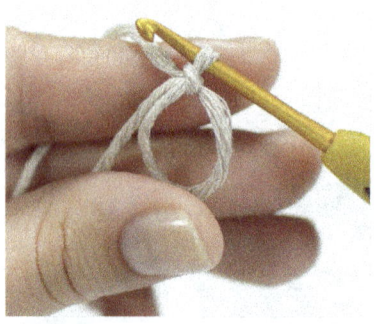

4. Pull the yarn tight. This does not count as the first stitch.

5. Hold the loop between your thumb and forefinger. Insert the hook through the loop from front to back.

6. Draw up a loop. Yarn over and draw through both loops on the hook, completing the first sc.

7. Continue crocheting through the loop and over the yarn tail until you have the required number of sc-s.

8. Hold the last stitch between your fingers, grab the yarn and pull ...

9. ... until the center is tightly closed.

72

Small Donkey | EN-084 | Copyright © 2019 Kristi Tullus | kristitullus.com

CHANGING YARNS

A quick and easy, but clean way to change yarns when working in single crochet stitch.

1. Stop before the last step of the last single crochet stitch with the "old" yarn.

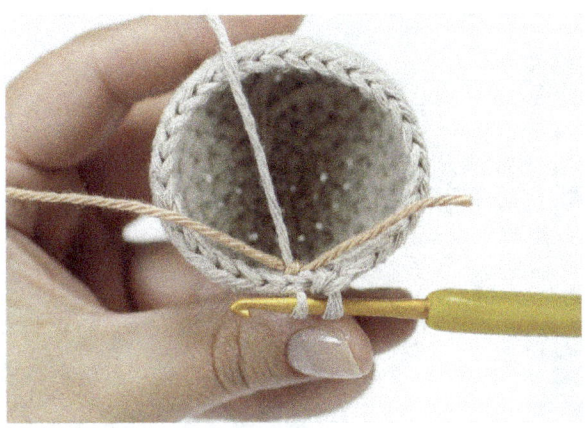

2. Tie the "new" yarn around the "old" yarn and push the knot close to the piece.

3. Cut the "old" yarn and knot the two yarn tails together.

4. Yarn over with the new yarn.

5. And draw through both loops on the hook, completing the single crochet stitch.

6. And then continue crocheting with the "new" yarn.

Small Donkey | EN-084 | Copyright © 2019 Kristi Tullus | kristitullus.com

INVISIBLE SINGLE CROCHET DECREASE

Pick up the front loops of both stitches and crochet one single crochet stitch into the loops. Alternatively you can replace it with a regular single crochet decrease.

1. Insert the hook under the front loop of the first single crochet stitch.

2. Insert the hook under the front loop of the second stitch and pick it up onto the hook.

3. Yarn over and draw through both loops on the hook. Yarn over ...

4. ... and draw through both loops on the hook, completing the single crochet stitch.

FINISHING AN OPEN PIECE

1. Finish the last stitch and then slip stitch in the next stitch.

2. Cut the yarn and fasten off.

3. Insert your hook through the next stitch, front to back.

4. And draw the yarn tail through. If you want to use the yarn tail for sewing, stop here.

5. Go through the next stitch, back to front.

6. And draw the yarn tail through. Now you can hide it inside the piece.

SEWING AN OPEN PIECE TO A CLOSED PIECE WITH WHIP STITCH

When you finish the open piece, leave a long yarn tail for sewing, and then fasten off.

1. Thread the yarn tail onto a needle. Insert the needle below the yarn tail and bring it up under the next stitch.

2. Draw the stitch tight.

3. Go through the next stitch front to back, inserting the needle under both loops.

4. Go back into the same hole you brought the yarn up last time and bring it up under the next stitch. Draw the stitch tight.

5. Or you can go through the stitch back to front, inserting the needle under both loops.

6. Draw the yarn through.

7. Go back into the same hole you brought the yarn up last time and bring it up under the next stitch. Draw the stitch tight.

8. Keep stitching, repeating steps 3 - 4 or 5 - 7 and go all around the open piece.

SEWING AN OPEN PIECE TO A CLOSED PIECE WITH MATTRESS STITCH

When you finish the open piece, leave a long yarn tail for sewing, and then fasten off.

1. Thread the yarn tail onto a needle. Insert the needle below the yarn tail and bring it up under the next stitch.

2. Draw the yarn through.

3. Insert the needle under the vertical bar of the next stitch.

4. Draw the yarn through.

5. Go back in the same hole where you brought the yarn up last time and bring it up under the next stitch.

6. Draw the yarn through.

7. Keep repeating steps 3 - 6.

8. Make a couple of stitches. Then grab the yarn tail and draw the stitches as tight as you can.

9. Go around the open piece, drawing the yarn tight after every couple of stitches.

FASTENING AND HIDING YARN TAILS

The quickest way to hide yarn tails is to just weave it through the stuffing a couple of times, going in different directions. But if you want to make it extra secure, you can tie the yarn around one of the loops of a stitch and then hide it inside the piece.

1. Bring the yarn up through a hole in the fabric.

2. Insert the needle under one loop of a stitch right next to the hole.

3. Pull until you have a small loop.

4. Knot the loop and yarn together, making a double knot. Do not push the first knot too close to the fabric.

5. Cut off the loop end.

6. Insert the needle into the same hole, going up and through the piece.

7. Pull lightly until the knot disappears into the fabric.

8. Cut off the yarn close to the fabric.

9. Yarn tail will completely disappear into the fabric.

www.ingramcontent.com/pod-product-compliance
Lightning Source LLC
Chambersburg PA
CBHW080022110526
44587CB00021BA/3735